MW00883648

THE NAPLES OF ENGLAND

ANDY CHRISTOPHER MILLER has worked as a professor of educational psychology for two British universities and published ten books in his field including *Child and Adolescent Therapy* (1992) and *Teachers, Parents and Classroom Behaviour: A Psychosocial Approach* (2003). He has also published book chapters, magazine and journal articles on topics as diverse as relationships, travel and mountaineering. A selection of these pieces, including his prize-winning poem for the 2011 Yeovil Literary Prize, was published as *While Giants Sleep* (2015).

What reviewers have said about Andy Miller's writing:

"… a distinctive voice …" DAISY GOODWIN, YEOVIL LITERARY PRIZE JUDGE

"… a terrific writer …" JOHN LINDLEY, CHESHIRE POET LAUREATE 2004

"… pulses with life and energy …" ALY STONEMAN, LEFT LION, NOTTINGHAM

"… moving, funny and compelling …" MEGAN TAYLOR, AUTHOR, 'THE LIVES OF GHOSTS'

"… superbly written …" DR PHIL STRINGER, EDUCATIONAL PSYCHOLOGY IN PRACTICE

"… elegantly crafted …" PROF NORAH FREDERICKSON, THE PSYCHOLOGIST

"… there is a breath of humanity in this book …" ED DRUMMOND, POET, ACTIVIST AND LEADING BRITISH ROCK CLIMBER

"… the best writing I've read for ages …" PROF TERRY GIFFORD, DIRECTOR, INTERNATIONAL FESTIVAL OF MOUNTAINEERING LITERATURE

THE NAPLES OF ENGLAND

Andy Christopher Miller

Amcott Press

Published by Amcott Press
68 The Dale
Wirksworth
Derbyshire
DE4 4EJ

The names of people and locations used in this book are pseudonyms

www.andycmiller.co.uk

THE NAPLES OF ENGLAND

1946 – 1965

Safe as Houses	9
When the Music Stops	13
Message in a Bottle	17
Common Knowledge	23
Every Sparrow Fallen	29
One for a Jack	35
In Scarlet Town	41
Pecking Order	45
The Naples of England	51
Like Survivors	59
Only a Book	67
Mentors for the Atomic Age	73
Racing Right Away	83
Fifty Miles is a Long Way	89
Telling You How to Live	97
Gainful Employment	103
Above and Beyond	113
Concrete Proposal	121

1983 – 1987

As Long As Everyone's Alright	131
Neither Shape Nor Shadow	141
Acknowledgements	*150*

1946 – 1965

Safe as Houses

'It was them ruddy Japs,' my mother said.

Johnny Forrest's dad was slap bang in the middle of the road right outside our house.

'They were cruel devils, they tortured their prisoners,' she added.

He was 'a nice fella', Johnny Forrest's dad, my Mum said. But now he was red-faced and raging at the top of his voice. Normally, he was softly spoken and polite. Today it was forbidden swear words and little else.

'That's how it left poor devils like him'.

There was nobody there as the obvious recipient of his anger and our neighbours were all indoors avoiding their windows.

'Come away. Somebody will fetch him'.

Usually, though, a comfortable web of activity surrounded our lives at number 100 Purbeck Road. A green double-decker bus, on route to the King's Statue down on the seafront, grumbled past our house, shuddering with its gear change just before the entrance to The Rec, on the hour, at twenty past and at twenty to.

The road sweeper made sleepy brush strokes along the gutter outside our hedge on hot summer days. From about the age of four, I would rush for my mother's broom if I heard his metal barrow clanking along the road. I followed behind him as his apprentice providing the finishing touches and was rewarded with elegant piles of sandy dust, twigs, leaves, lollipop sticks, cigarette packets and matchboxes.

Another regular along Purbeck Road in the years before I went to school, was Mrs Crosby, the afternoon paper lady. Whatever the weather, she wore a headscarf and gabardine coat stained and stiffened by newsprint. Bent in upon herself, with a hooked nose, and hurried, indistinct vocalisations, she wheeled a daily bulk of South Dorset Gazettes in a baby's pram. I used to frequently ask my mother if I could help Mrs Crosby and was told that I must not make a nuisance of myself. Like a tiresome dog that brings back a stick too quickly, I would be at her side asking for another paper to deliver, making more work than I spared her.

The baker made a perfunctory bread delivery at mid-morning every day and the Co-op grocery boxes arrived each Tuesday. My mother seemed a little ill at ease with the eager banter from the bespectacled, lanky man who brought these provisions, who actually stepped inside the back door to place the heavy cardboard boxes directly onto the top of our kitchen cupboard.

For me, the most exciting of the street-based merchants who trekked across the Shorehaven estate was the fishmonger. His heavy wooden barrow, with swinging pails of fish and sculpted weighing scales with iron weights, creaked along our road in the early morning. His cry, intriguing but also, like Mrs Crosby's diction, menacing in its indecipherability, would sometimes wake me on summer days. Fresh West Bay mackerel, caught during the night, were announced in a voice growing louder as it approached.

'Wheeeeeeeey…..Krull!'

The surprise breakfasts that followed, the meaty aroma imperious about the kitchen, the salty sea filtered through the fibrous flesh. Like childhood itself, never as immediate again, never so exquisitely recaptured.

There were the less-told tales though, the ones reserved for my times alone with my mother. Her voice would drop to a heavy whisper with breathy emphasis. Her shoulders became hunched as if she had to shake the most distressing words from her lips by means of a rapid, sideways shaking of her head.

'Those camps, when we saw them on the newsreels at the pictures after the war, I just couldn't believe it. Belsen. Those wretches, they weren't human. All skin and bone. Couldn't walk some of them, had to be carried. Like skeletons. I couldn't bear to look, couldn't get it out of my head. I kept seeing them for ages.'

Vivid, all around her for my mother. It was the lived present. The panorama and the spectacle of war, the defiant rhetoric of Winston Churchill. The huge, shared purpose. The horrors, the moments when the restraint slipped. The persistent and recurring memories.

All in the past for me. Before my birth, before my life. It was history, as were cavemen and Romans. I was born at the beginning of a New Age. 1946. The world had been scoured, scorched and cleansed at a terrible cost. Chance had chosen me and my generation to be its most fortunate beneficiaries.

When the Music Stops

'Hold his feet. Somebody get his feet'.

'Ooof!'

Clanking machinery somewhere out of sight jolting my padded chair another notch upwards, the Big Wheel's juddering progress towards the sky. My arms held down by my side, then my legs, the rubber mask pressing ever more firmly into my face. A last intake of breath, clawing at the oxygen. Its effects easily spent, the steady hiss from the machine overpowering my rhythms. A final wrench of one shoulder, twisting at the waist, firmly pushed back and pinned down. My hold on the present weakening further and then extinguishing. Echoing voices, metal implements, searchlights brought down closer, thick fingers on my face then in my mouth, the sensations becoming vaguer as I float upwards in the huge chair. Heavy, scraping levers, rusty cog wheels misaligned and almost falling to connect. The huge arc swept out by my oppressors, their cold technology and me slumped in my chair, moving together slowly through one whole revolution. The friction from a brake as if burning against iron, the circular momentum restrained, the click and clang as we become stationary and level with the room again, the bolts locking us securely back on firm ground. Blood in my mouth.

'That's it, good boy. All done. Have a rinse and a spit in here if you want to'.

There was a choice at the dentists, gas or cocaine. Both had their detractors, each their horrible mythologies. For me, being smothered into sleep seemed preferable to the needle in the jaw. Victor Critchley had shown me with his hands the length of the needle that had punctured his brother's mouth. It must have been driven, eight inches or more, through the thin strip of gum, through upper tooth and bone, on into the soft cerebral tissues and finally out through his eggshell scalp and tangled hair into the daylight. The dentist was inescapable with surprise school inspections sprung upon us at various ages. The agents of the State, we knew, maintained scrupulous records in which any absentees were noted, to be followed up by personalised appointments delivered in official brown envelopes to our very homes by their tireless ally, the postman.

Our docility and captivity within school were exploited again and again. Cycling proficiency tests were inescapable for all bicycle owners. White-coated doctors, the most feared of all, descended and appropriated corridors and offices seemingly without challenge. Whatever they required was provided and we stood anxiously in line for them, bragging, tearful or fighting back the terror.

'When you're in the fourth year they come and you have to cough or something and then they touch you on your balls,' or so the rumour went.

Greater than these terrors though was the communal care provided us. The children's section of Weymouth public library, although hushed and proper in tone, let us loose amongst its vast bounty. Huge school dinners - carrots, peas, gravy, suet and pastry, pies, puddings and custard. Women who lived on the Shorehaven estate, our near neighbours, reappeared at lunchtimes in the school hall dressed in overalls, cheerfully plying us with food, judging the most deserving for the 'seconds' queue, on rare occasions even signaling with wide eyes the opportunities for third helpings. Then afterwards we were led into the school hall and seated cross-legged on the polished, springy floor to listen to radio programmes created especially for us. Mounted up towards the ceiling, large varnished speakers with circular golden grills beamed down reassuring voices into the hall.

'Hello children. Do you remember the song we have been learning about a sixpence? When the music stops Uncle Brian will be here to teach you the next verse'.

Each note from the piano reverberated around the room, haunting harmonics high in the hall. Occasionally children slumped to the floor to be scooped into a more comfortable position by patrolling teachers, even covered with small blankets in winter, while the rest of us were entranced further by the respectable, measured diction coming from the speakers. Our teachers and these kindly broadcasters in an easy partnership, furthering our nurture.

We would not go hungry. We would be comforted.

We were to be protected from preventable disease.

We were to aspire. We were to have knowledge and then to know even more, right out to the very boundaries if we wished.

Message in a Bottle

Turrets and battlements crafted with patience and precision. Corridors and cloisters, enclosed and open stairways, a working drawbridge and a keep, all fashioned with affection. The fort that Grandad Miller made for me as a Christmas present when I was eight years old was perfect.

I associated Grandad with Christmas because of it and the fact that he and Granny usually visited us on that day. Granny Miller wasn't my Dad's real mother, I knew that. She was Sam's second wife, my Dad's step-mother. Somehow, this rested sensibly within the order of things. Some people had mothers, others stepmothers, and my Dad had one of the latter.

The Granny Miller I had known was a full square person. I remember her in her Christmas Day best, black and shapeless, with straight and fine grey hair, cut at an even length. When I had not seen her for a while, she merged with the fearsome Giles granny in my father's Daily Express and, from my mother's anxiety before her visits, I knew there must be some justification for this comparison.

My mother, on her way home from town once, had called in on Granny to ask whether she needed anything fetching from the shops, only to come away with admonition stinging in her ears. She had two young boys at home needing looking after, what was she thinking about wandering around town and calling in on people? Keeping a cautionary eye on her when we were together, I avoided her wrath, never falling within its orbit nor, to be fair, witnessing any of its beginnings. Smoking her Senior Service, talking in an intriguingly deep and matter of fact voice, like a man, downbeat and cynical sometimes, she also kept an agreeable distance from me.

Grandad was altogether different, in appearance small and wiry and in manner, watchful, appreciative and understated. Nowadays, the contrasts might be readily noticed. Back then, and to me, people existed in each other's presence and that was that. Compatibility was not a notion that I heard entertained.

'She was lucky to get him, she was only an old washerwoman from Fleet after all really,' my mother explained.

When they visited on Christmas Day my mother would wash up after lunch while Granny slept in front of the fire. I found having to suppress my amusement at her whistling breath and occasional abrupt snorts excruciating.

The four of us males, my grandfather, father, my brother and I, would get the table ready, then cut, shuffle and deal the cards - the ritual opening of the pontoon game.

'Have you got your money then Grandad?' my father would goad.

'What about you two, are you alright?' he would ask, turning to us, knowing that we could not be this close and still be unprepared.

When we were younger we had played for matchsticks but now that I was about to leave primary school, we were allowed halfpenny stakes, - 'a penny maximum!' We had left behind the make-believe, now there was the sweat and dirty copper of real currency.

Grandad smoked Capstan Full Strength and said very little.

'What are you doing, sticking?'

He never removed the cigarette from his lips, allowing

the wonderful architecture of the ash to bend towards collapse by minute degrees, while opaque blue and grey serpents wreathed about his head, some disappearing into his nostrils like sleek and eager parasites. He studied his cards to the exclusion of us all. I thought, at times when the smoke diminished, that he might be minimally moving his head as if reckoning his hand.

My father always pushed for a brisker pace.

'What have you got there? Seventeen? What are you doing, sticking?'

Nothing. An intake of breath, words possibly struggling to form in the tiny movements of his head. Then nothing again.

'He's got seventeen. Haven't you?'

I wondered about Grandad's supposed deafness. How could we really know whether my Dad's raised voice was in any way more effective? Perhaps, there would be no communication until we all shouted our every word or used metal cones as loud hailers, like in the Beano.

'He can hear all right. He's just acting daft. You can hear, can't you? What is it, seventeen? Sticking, aren't you?'

Then the delicious reward. Grandad would emerge from the smoke, from his silence, from the darkening afternoon.

'Eh?'

'What are you doing? Come on, buying, twisting or sticking? Let's be having you.'

I would be animated on my chair. My father would ask me once more to stop wriggling, but as the possibility of entering another, even more protracted cycle looked ever more likely, there was no place to turn from the tension. Nobody could leave the table to switch on the light. Granny might at times shuffle herself. My mother might quietly enter the room and take a chair. The gloom would add an increasingly despairing dimension.

And then he threw a halfpenny across the table. After all this he was buying.

'Buying on seventeen? What you got there then, fifteen?'

The most superficial glance at his new card and another halfpenny flew across the table with the same apparent disinterest.

'Bust?' said my father, confident in his challenge once Grandad had turned the corner of this final card.

'Stick!'

He'd done it and it was wonderful, better than anything on our new television, and he defeated all my watchful scrutiny. Neither could I discern the extent of my father's possible complicity. No scripted performances could evoke from me such a longing for resolution. A playful wink just to me would have been a Christmas present indeed. The old magician and his cloak, the illusion of being slow-witted and deliberate, no let up, lost endlessly in oriental seascapes for all any of us knew.

Grandad had been a sailor in the Merchant Navy, finishing his working life as a stoker on the Channel Islands paddle steamers. When he was approaching sixty five, the shipping company told him that he would soon be too old to be shovelling coke down in the furnace room. It was time to think about retirement. Leave all that bending to younger men and enjoy the salty spittle upright in the outdoors. He protested that the work was not beyond him and demonstrated that, with the cigarette gripped in his mouth and proving no hindrance, he was the better of any of them. Hardly speaking among the high piles of coke, sweating and steady-footed in rolling seas, he was completely at home with the huge bellied forces of fire and steam.

But he was made to retire nonetheless and sadly, quietly accepted what he would have felt to be a great betrayal of his loyalty and resolution.

My father said that Grandad walked at an angle, leaning over to one side, because he had spent so much of his life at sea. I sometimes spotted him from the top of our bus coming over Westgate Bridge, hurrying towards town where he had a new evenings and mornings job, clearing up the glasses after hours in the basement bar of the Glengary Hotel up on the seafront. The story was that, although a Guinness drinker by nature, he went around the tables clearing sops of many varieties by drinking them, unable just to pour them down the sink. Off to work at ten thirty at night, home at around quarter to one, then back to clean up first thing in the morning ready for a brand new subterranean day. With all the leftovers he could drink and the opportunity to be helpful, my father said it was the ideal retirement for him.

I called on him on my way home from town once or twice and was not sent away. Following him one morning when I was nine or ten from the front door, through the dark hallway where musty coats hung, into the back parlour, he said

'You've come at the right time'.

On the table was a large whiskey bottle on its side and inside a mess of wood, fabric and waxed twine. 'Watch this,' he said, steadying his breathing to control against any cloud of smoke from his cigarette that might obscure his eye line. Carefully, the tiny muscles around his mouth regulating his efforts, he drew towards him the threads hanging from the bottle's neck and the muddle of its contents began to move, began to assert itself into the full blossoming of a rigged ship in sail - decks, masts, canvas against the wind, ropes taking the tension.

He let out a small breath, a pinched but deep satisfaction. There was nothing here that words could improve upon although they tumbled out from me indiscriminately. He said nothing in reply, either absorbing or deflecting my gabble, but smiled and nodded at the bottle in front of him on the table. In this dull back room, with treacle-like varnish on the panelled wall that held in the stairs, I had seen the birth of a morning at sea, fuelled with enough confidence for a full circumnavigation, able to hold a determined course beneath the most perverse or alien of constellations.

Common Knowledge

'Quick! It's that bloke!'

Kids scattered like minnows towards their gardens and back doors.

'Who is he?' I asked, watching the big man as he shambled up the road towards us, his head rolling slowly from side to side like that of a burdened beast.

'He gives you stuff if you go down his house with him. Money and stuff. But he ties you up and takes your trousers off,' explained Ricky, before darting down the alleyway that led to his own back garden.

I was indoors immediately, past my parents and up crouching beneath the window of my bedroom, blood racing, cramped down so that my back could not possibly show above the sill. I waited and counted, counted and waited, wanting to be sure that when I did raise my head to look, the man would be past our house and along towards the other end of the road, not leaning against the lamp post opposite with eyes fixed on my bedroom window. I was terrified that when I did finally raise my head above the sill, the man would be right there, ready to lock my gaze.

All the kids had heard of 'funny men' and their descriptions were passed down by those more 'in the know,' or at least seemingly so. Likewise, although actual encounters were rare, we had all absorbed the rumours about favoured haunts and remained watchful.

But on a previous occasion, news had spread that a funny man had been approaching kids down at the Sports Field. Bored and looking for excitement, I tagged along with a large group who decided to seek him out in a game of real stakes pursuit.

'We're safe as long as we all stick together,' said Ricky.

It was never a consideration, of course, that any of us would tell our parents. What vocabulary, beyond the excruciatingly rude and embarrassing, could we have possibly employed?

The Field covered a larger area than the Rec. It bordered the golf course and was marked out in football pitches complete with goal posts. Many adventures and explorations started here. Going 'out across' entailed disappearing from the everyday adult world at the far end of the Sports Field by sliding down Slippery Slope, the mud bank opening in the bramble-covered hillside.

But on that particular day we were highly vigilant. Some of us had much younger brothers and sisters to take care of, little ones whose acceleration if suddenly required was much in doubt. We trekked across likely openings and clearings like flirtatious fawns, nonchalant but calculating bait.

And suddenly he was there, a small man in a raincoat and beret, smiling down on us, leering from the top of Slippery Slope. Carol Devaney screamed, unsettling everybody, and began to run, pulling her tiny sister along the track beside the Reed Bed, around the Newt Pond and on into the interior. Rattling with terror, I became every hero I had ever encountered, each surging within me and then immediately gone. I wanted to shepherd the slow ones but also save my own skin, to regroup in some corner and discover our collective strength yet also skim swiftly, alone and unhindered, across the long grass.

We evaded the man, stopped running and stopped shaking. Some started to cry, others became wild and argumentative. We agreed again to stick together, to move at the same speed, scouts focusing on the way ahead while others consolidated the ground already covered. And in this way we secured safe passage back from the limits of our known world towards the familiarity of footballers' cries from across the Sports Field and then into Oakcroft Avenue where police and parental jurisdiction once again prevailed.

But today this huge man who was walking with impunity down our very street carried a far heavier menace and brought it right up to our front door. In my bedroom I calculated the amount of time the man would take to pass the house and then doubled that before risking a look. Raising my head just enough to be above the window sill, I saw him well advanced down the road, nearing the corner with Cheviot Street. He was by the gate of the house where Janet Aston, my second cousin, lived. Janet was in the same class as me at school and was straight-backed and plain with limp fair hair often tied in bunches. I never spoke to her though nor told anybody that we were somehow related. In fact, my family never exchanged more than a passing pleasantry with Janet's. She wasn't allowed to play out with the others. They were Jehovah's Witnesses.

At their gate, Janet's dad, still in his work overalls, was shaking his fist at the monster in their road. My Dad reckoned that Janet's father was alright as long as he never tried to inflict his religion onto others. I could not see Mr Aston's face clearly enough but his stance and movements were unusual, outside the standard repertoire of anger. What had Janet told her father to raise such ferocity? Even though I had been assured that they were a strange family, I could not believe that she had dared to tell what the other kids had told me.

The apparent heroism on her father's part, and my disbelief that the unspeakable could have in fact been uttered, were somehow compromised by what I knew of the family.

Sometimes Jehovah's Witnesses called at our own house, causing my Dad to struggle with the stiffness of the infrequently opened, heavy front door.

'Good morning, we wondered if you are concerned like we are about all the –'

'Yes, thank you very much,' my father would say or almost sing, interrupting them.

'The Lord – '.

'Yes, thank you'.

Bang! The door was shut.

It seemed to me like a sort of heroism as I watched my father walk back down the passage to carry on mixing the batter for Sunday dinner Yorkshire puddings. He sometimes announced with great approval that there had been two forbidden topics of conversation in the RAF mess in the war - politics and religion.

'People would start arguing the toss and it would always end in trouble,' he explained when I asked him why. But how his closing the door like that could really be bravery puzzled me, complicated as it was by what seemed like rudeness in the interrupting, in not letting the callers finish their piece. And anyway, the war had been over now for the whole ten years of my life.

Mr Aston was out there in the road, in full sight of everybody, directly challenging the beast-like man. This should have seemed heroic too but, because Mr Aston was already seen to be outside the swim of the everyday social world, I struggled to construe him in so positive a light. Better instead to see these combatants as two outcasts together, two disturbers of the peace. Their tussle could tip them over the side of the world, into the void and beyond view. The people on our road, on the whole Shorehaven estate even, would then be restored and relieved, absolved and freed from further consternation.

Every Sparrow Fallen

Lizards, snakes, frogs and newts.

We were custodians of the hedgerows, the waterlogged bomb site and the waste ground. Inside the old air raid shelter, erratic movements up the wall. In the dark, among the rubble underfoot, something slithering resentfully away. Turning over large rocks or abandoned sheets of galvanised roofing panel, millipedes, spiders or slow worms writhing and dissipating in all directions into the surrounding grass. If we were really lucky, a lordly grass snake or evil-eyed adder.

For me, an implicit and approximate understanding of the evolutionary ladder was also my yardstick for empathy. Molluscs, insects, things without legs, if they did not cause me fear, elicited contempt. One of my earliest memories was of playing in a friend's garden and setting out to rid his parents of the pestilence of cabbage white caterpillars. We enlisted the help of other kids in picking them from the stems and undersides of wrinkled brassica leaves while I climbed onto their garden shed, a brick built construction with a rounded metal roof and a chimney. I bent to receive each offering from the others with cupped hands and then, for some reason, dropped them down the chimney. After every half a dozen or so such manoeuvres I also dropped a rock or broken house brick after them with a grandiose sense of adult importance. I found this complicated method of dispatch thrilling, my sense of dispassionate and mechanised efficiency grossly alluring.

Ants, by contrast, were a far more advanced and civilised species than caterpillars, spectacular though the cycle of cocoon, dry chrysalis and eventual, flowering emergence as a butterfly always proved to be. Colonies of ants lived under the path in our back garden and I was intrigued by their intricate collaborations. They dragged objects in convoy and patiently reorganised, without a visible language or method of signalling, to surmount the various obstacles with which I sought to test their invisible ingenuity.

Occasionally though, I showered them with cascades of boiling water. They were a pest and I willed myself insensitive to their imagined screaming and gloated in the adult conversations I had with myself - thinking about it not getting the job done, being cruel to be kind. At one moment entranced with being omnipotent and alive. Later, shamed, disgusted and frightened by the delight and the delusion of necessity with which I had carried out such unpitying destruction.

Set against this though, I was capable of being deeply distressed by the suffering of animals and birds. At nine years old I carried a badly wounded house sparrow in a shoebox on two buses, one to the seafront then another along Dorchester Road, to secure its relief from a vet. I returned empty-handed biting back tears, wondering whether the bird really could be saved by the gentle professionalism of the staff – 'they always die' was the view I heard often enough, - but also reliving time and again their warm and reassuring attention towards me.

Separated from adults, we children shared a different sentient world with creatures of the wild. We patrolled the hawthorn, bramble and sedge. Rare sightings were rumoured, the secret locations of nests traded. We depleted the clusters of warmed and speckled eggs responsibly, just one for a collection, secure in Nature's effortless abundance and its unending replenishment.

But to be included, or at least to wander the estate and

fields free from ambush and attack, required the suppression of some sensibilities. The older kids with air rifles could serve as protectors or as patrolling vigilantes. I became craven, wretched in muted collusion, behind Victor Critchley's hedge one night as his older brother lined up his sights with the ridge along their roof top. Like a pack of hunters finely attuned to each other's silences, we watched the line of sparrows and starlings squabbling and chattering along the tiles. Pfft! An instant space in the line as the other birds shrieked into the air. Not the zing of spinning tin as at the Fair, rustlers with sly grins in neckerchiefs or Indians with tomahawks. Just a puff of feathered life no more, the slick reloading routine, the muttered acknowledgement of the shot among the older kids.

Greater horrors were related though thankfully never witnessed. The boy, a friendless, spiteful character plucking out the eyes of live baby birds from the nests. Like picking winkles to eat from their shells with a pin but cruel, merciless and cold. After I had been told this, the image would sometimes resurface as I tried to get to sleep at night. I believed that if I never solidified these awful images with my own spoken words then their intrusions would eventually cease. But although unvoiced they still returned and some nights I had to press my own eyeballs in hard with my knuckles to suppress the thoughts and hold myself intact.

When I was nine my Aunt Jocelyn came to stay with us for a few days. On other occasions, Uncle Sid came by himself because they were unable to both leave behind their dog on its own. My aunt's visits were anticipated by my parents with a dizzyingly high degree of anxiety. My father seemed to increase the amount of overtime he worked when she visited and I was aware of the snatched conversations between my mother and her, worrying away in corners, fast, hushed and watchful, biting back into silence if I approached.

On this occasion, Aunt Jocelyn asked if she could bring the dog with her. She warned us that it could get 'over-excited' but I saw this as no impediment. The vagaries of animal nature were a daily wonder to me and the search for authoritative but reassuring responses one of life's more welcome challenges. I assured my parents that I would be privileged to take on the major responsibility for the animal's welfare and amusement if it was allowed to come.

Whether or not this was a deciding factor, I never learned. But the visit took place, aunt and dog together, and on the second night of their stay I was granted a wish greater than I could have hoped for. My aunt and mother had tickets for a show on the pier and had to be out of the house half an hour before my father returned home from work. I assured them that my brother and the dog would be safe in my charge and my mother insisted I locked the door immediately they left and opened it to nobody until my father arrived.

As they stepped out and closed the door behind them, I shivered with pride and a giddy sense of autonomy. But before the door could click closed behind them, before I could shoot the bolts, the dog ran at it and then along the hall to the front without stopping. It hit each door with a full force thud, scrabbled back to its sliding feet, claws flailing against the lino, and wailed dementedly. It barked sharply then careered straight into me, unreachable by command or consolation. As I struggled to my feet to follow, it was upstairs in three bounds, skidding at speed through the landing, bouncing in flight momentarily on my bed like a trampolinist garnering momentum, and then on sailing out through the open window into the warm evening air of Purbeck Road, a howling, convulsing mess of limbs, rigid and broken, down before me on our front lawn.

One for a Jack

My mother used to say that I wasn't to go bothering Mrs James, that we had to leave our neighbours in peace sometimes, but every time I knocked on her door it was obvious that she was pleased to see me.

I always asked whether she would like a game of 'Beat Jack Out of Doors' and every time she stopped what she was doing and beckoned me into her gloomy back room which was heavy with large and serious furniture. She always brought a plate of luxury biscuits in from the kitchen, macaroons with rice paper or chocolate digestives. She would play her hand carefully and lay down any cards she had to forfeit in an unhurried fashion - one for a Jack of mine, two for a Queen and so on.

'Come again, Andrew. I'm always pleased to see you, my dear,' she would say when I left. Or something like that, definitely proving my mother wrong.

I had known Mr James too before he died. I used to watch him over our back garden fence, a respectable and kindly spaceman in his beekeeper's apparel.

'Don't get too close now,' he once said. 'They can get upset if there's any change to their routine'.

And they certainly could. It was actually something as small as a bee sting that ended up killing him one Sunday afternoon when I was ten.

I was playing with some of the other kids up on The Rec. Three of us were lying flat on a swing each and twisting the chains so that we would be swung round and made dizzy when we raised our feet from the ground. Because it was a Sunday I wasn't allowed out for so long but I had been to church that morning with my mother so there was no Sunday School and I knew I could stay until four o'clock.

That's why it was a surprise when my Dad appeared at the corner before it was even three.

'It's your Dad, Andy,' Ricky said and I ran to him, curious about his presence. It wasn't teatime, there were no visits planned and I had fulfilled my religious observances.

'Come on home,' he said 'Right now, I want you at home'.

My father always walked at a furious pace and when I sometimes accompanied him to or from his bus stop on workday lunchtimes, I enjoyed the absurdity of trying to move at such a speed, the sight of his arms and legs in such animation, me having to burst into a run to keep up and maintain our conversation.

But that Sunday afternoon he was so clipped in his speech, with the sense of a coldness only one unnecessary question from me away. I walked as fast as I could behind him, as he powered himself back along the pavement to our house, wondering what misdemeanour of mine had been detected. With an increasing sense of fear, and desperate to confess and relieve the tension, I ran through the various arenas in which I might be at fault - school, the spelling test, my brother, my mum. But I couldn't think of anything serious enough to warrant this, anything that could have come suddenly to light in the middle of a Sunday afternoon.

Indoors my mother looked at me but said nothing. There was no way I could get her alone to ask her what was happening, to tell her that I had done nothing wrong.

'Go up to your bedroom,' my father said and, as he caught me looking towards my mother, trying to demand her intervention, he seemed sharper still.

'Do what you're told. Right now!'

From my bedroom, I could hear no sounds within the house. Silence and a sense of absence played about the walls, carpet and linoleum. I had seldom been punished in such a way and was unable to predict the likely duration nor what might happen next.

Then later there were quiet voices in the street, or possibly in our garden. I heard the door of a vehicle being closed, these muffled sounds coming to me through the airbrick high up in my bedroom wall. I opened the door handle through the smallest of fractions, trying to avoid the sprung click of the latch echoing through the hallway like the smack of a stick on a snare drum. Pacing around the creaky floorboards that I knew could be heard from downstairs, I made a careful journey all the way to the window at the end of our L-shaped landing.

There was an ambulance outside next door's gate, outside Mr and Mrs James' house, and the discrete conversation and business-like movements of the two uniformed men seemed adult and thrilling. Next door's back door was ajar. I could hear my parents downstairs. I knew that I should retreat to my bedroom with care but moved with a faster foot, taking more risks. I lay on my bed, drawn deeply into the mystery. The solemnity and the ruptured Sunday afternoon were clearly bound up with the presence of the ambulance. There was an agitation in the air - ambulances glided through our estate only in the most serious of circumstances - but also the beginnings of happiness and relief, a growing expectation that I was not in trouble after all.

When my mother came and told me that I could go back downstairs, she hurried on ahead of me, not available for my questions. In the kitchen the electric oven was heating up. The earthenware mixing bowl was on the side and my father was making a Victoria sponge. He excelled at these, and made great play about the necessity for the oven to be hot enough. My brother had been in his bedroom too and my mother told us both that Mr James had had an accident, that he had been stung by one of his bees.

Stings, cuts, grazes and bruises were the currency of my childhood explorations, a commonplace among the fields and brambles. The oven hummed, its loose handle buzzing as the temperature crept upwards. My father's jollity and busyness lifted any remaining gloom. The electric light was switched on, obliterating the last trace of dinginess. The oven's warmth enriched the kitchen and the smell of the rising cake, the sense of a nourishing presence, cheered the whole room, passing on into the passage, the stairway and even the upstairs landing.

A day or two later I was informed that Mr James had died - from a bee sting – or, more precisely, from the heart attack it had triggered. The hives that bordered our back garden were dismantled and removed by men from the council while I was at school a few days later. And, although I dreaded meeting Mrs James across the fence straight afterwards, it felt very important to see again the spot where the colony of bees had lived, to know the exact coordinates of death. Only two rusty wires sagging between cast concrete posts separated this fundamental event from the unstoppable germination and growth within our own garden.

But somehow this incident had already lost its power.

One for a Jack.

New day had formed over the past.

Two for a Queen.

The future was already present.

In Scarlet Town

'Andrew Miller, go outside! Outside that door! Immediately!'

'What did you think you were doing?'

(There had been no thought.)

'Whatever were you trying to do?'

(No intention either. No plan.)

'Whatever possessed you?

(Nothing had taken hold of me.)

Except, perhaps, the rush of the music and the pounding of the dance. Like a dog biting the wind or barking at the intensity of the moment.

I had been taken up in the immediacy, the impulse, and couldn't say why I had tripped Julie Dyson. I certainly couldn't explain it then and I'm not sure I can offer anything more tangible even now.

I do know that I was extremely ill at ease during our singing lessons. It was something about the language, arcane and respectable, and the constant reproaches.

'Hold your head up when you sing. And stop slouching and mumbling!'

In Scarlet Town where I was born
There was a fair maid dwelling

'Pull your shoulders back. And smile. For heaven's sake, smile!'

Made every lad cry 'Well a-day'
For love of Barbara Allen.

Far, far worse though was the country dancing.

Boys and girls on opposite sides of the hall in equal numbers.

'Now choose a partner. Quickly, and without any fuss.'

The one or two boys who had a cousin in the class were the most fortunate. They approached quietly and claimed a hand to the relief of both partners. Next the footballers, their easy confidence less prominent indoors but still pronounced enough to lead them towards the prettier of the girls. And last of all, the biggest group in a desperate, uncertain scramble to avoid being left with Dora Bartholomew. Poor Dora, picking her nose, her regulation grey pullover clumsily darned at the elbows and hanging in stringy threads at the cuffs. Her pleated, bottle green skirt stained from a lunchtime spillage. And her smell. Resignation in her big, dull eyes, like an old, sad beast in a pen, selected for slaughter.

Then the positioning, boys with their arms around their partner's waists.

'Count the beats and listen to the introduction. Wait for your cue. And … dance!'

Round we clumped, the music maintaining our momentum.

'Lift your knees up. Skip properly. Look as if you are enjoying yourself!'

Despite my distaste for the whole business, I found myself able to skip in time with the music if I gave it my full concentration. My partner's waist, however, kept slipping from my sweaty grip and I feared the impropriety of exercising too firm a hold on her. The fixed smile proved to be an additional challenge I was unable to meet.

After a long period of red-faced grimacing and galloping, we boys were asked to sit on the gymnasium benches around the side while the girls practiced their particular segment of a dance. Although I was relieved to be out of the arena, my pulse was still racing. We watched the girls circle the hall. More compliant than us, more genuine enjoyment in their step, more diligent concentration. I stuck out my foot.

Julie Dyson's sudden impact with my leg and then her two or three step stagger caused me panic. Her knees and hands crashing onto the springy floorboards reverberated through the hall, a terror choking my desperation to confess and be punished. Of all the girls, I had felled beautiful, straight-backed Julie Dyson. Julie who spoke in accents clear and still. Julie whom I sometimes stood behind in assembly admiring the clean symmetry of her neck muscles and the confident hang of her pony tail.

Oh let me see Thy footprints and in them plant mine own.
My hope to follow Julie is in Thy strength alone.

Outside the hall our teacher told me that my act would have serious consequences. Very serious consequences.

'You will be banned from country dancing lessons from today onwards!'

Banned.

'You will certainly not go to the country dancing county championships at Castle Carey in the summer. Everybody else will be going and you will be staying behind'.

The county championships.

'And I want you to come and see me at the staffroom at the end of afternoon playtime when I've had a chance to talk to the other teachers. Do you understand?'

Trembling inside and with my feelings hollowed out, I waited through the afternoon fearing the cane or the slipper. But instead, it had been decided that, while the rest of my class danced after lunch each Tuesday, I was to be Miss Chamberlain's sole companion in her classroom where I would write lines in silence and help her to make the teachers' tea before playtime.

I was ten and had never before made a cup of tea, at least not one that was drinkable. All I knew was that a procedure known as warming the pot was key. My mother gave me lessons at home while I implored her not to tell my father what we were doing or why.

Miss Chamberlain was an imposing woman who, in summer, wore large and shapeless floral print dresses. With a pronounced, masculine jaw she reminded me of Desperate Dan's wife. Her stoical manner suggested that she might not be the most popular of staffroom colleagues and the prospect of having to spend a weekly three quarters of an hour together, just her and me, was a worrying one. In the event, however, although she hardly spoke during our first session we seemed to find a comfortable distance as we pursued our separate endeavours. She was not unduly abrupt about my lack of competence when we made the tea in a large, aluminium teapot and as the weeks passed I settled into a relaxed and almost reassuring routine with her. Two outcasts going about our duties.

Removed from practice for the county championships, far away from the bright white plimsolls, the straightened socks, freshly-ironed white shirts and school ties, I was able to draw strength and a sense of engagement from a very different music caught occasionally on our radio at home – Bill Hayley, Elvis Presley and Chuck Berry.

Pecking Order

When I was nine years old my father surprised me by agreeing to the conversion of half of our shed into a pigeon loft, an action forbidden under the terms of our council tenancy. The shed was partitioned with wooden struts covered with chicken wire and into the roof a 'trap' was fitted whereby bent lengths of strong wire allowed entry into the shed from the outside but no return.

The true wonder of this shed, however, lay in the homing instincts of its occupants. Other kids gave me pigeons from their families' sheds and I soon established my own collection of five blue bars and one red. I was told that they would probably 'home' after being in their new coop for around three days and, despite fearing ridicule for my lack of patience, I risked my flock to the sky after two and a half. Not just to the immediate space where sunshine and light winds played against our own red brick walls, not just the line of rooftops curving away as Cheviot Road bent gently up hill, but to the whole sky, as vast as the estate and the town, and the open boundaries of the sea and hills that contained my sense of human scale and home.

And they came back. Although I had shaken the corn tin, whistled and called while they executed their swift, swerving patterns between the houses and their joyous high arcs against the blue sky, I knew they returned of their own volition. Some perched on rooftops overlooking the shed for a while, others delayed on the board outside the trap, jerking their heads back and forth. But they all stepped through the trap, the zinc-coated prongs rising across their shoulders as they entered, then falling shut with a thin clank behind them.

I showered them with the corn mixture, spraying their floor with my gratitude. Their freedom and captivity, my beneficence and control.

The greatest event though, something which seemed unsurpassed in my life, was the presence one morning of two white eggs in a clumsily constructed nest box. The slightly-built hen bird sitting on them seemed more alert than usual, and I willed these eggs to hatch, knowing from other boys that patience would be required for a full twenty one days. When had these been laid? Whilst I was asleep or indoors eating a meal?

Despite every warning about disturbing the nest too much, I checked these eggs for fractures a number of times a day, at breakfast time, after school and before going to bed. When a small chipped crack did eventually appear at the apex of one egg, I returned it quickly to the nest, but was back in the shed early the next morning. The crack had developed into fault lines forming three sides of a tiny, ragged square. I held the egg, willing the moment when this tiny trap door would creak open. I imagined my own limbs being folded and aligned, compacted inside exact curved surfaces. Suffocation and terrible constraint. Too tight to breathe, too tight to lever any force against the wall. And then I snicked away the flake of shell with the nail of my little finger.

Horrified at having interfered, instead of a chick bursting with a swagger, beak first out into the open, in the tiny aperture I could see only membrane and pink, under-prepared life. I placed the egg straight back with the other, asked the mother bird to return to the incubation and waited at the door until she did. After running home from school at the end of that day, I felt huge relief at seeing a much larger hole and a yellow beak, new and shiny like plastic, and I left well alone. By the next morning, the baby bird, with sealed eyes and heavy clumsy beak was half out, sitting in the remaining shell as if its broad bottom were wedged inside the bowl.

Both eggs hatched, and nothing in my days equalled the thrill of watching the industry of both parent birds, back and forth, filling their crops with food and regurgitating it into the open beaks of their offspring. Whilst the other pigeons strutted on their perches, even squabbled occasionally over ascendancy, and took the flights I offered them, this all now seemed perfunctory. The up-turned beaks, the screeching at the approach of the parents, the unconsidered purpose in the short repetitive journeys, these seemed to me the obvious priorities of the community.

Almost from hatching, one chick grew bigger than the other. Blind, with only rudimentary stubble where their feathers would grow, their lumpy bodies were more fluid than flesh. The larger bird, at first, had the air of a protective companion, as both were squashed beneath the nesting mother's feathers or were left looking out into the loft, awkward and lost, while their parents flew or fed. But within the nest box itself, a pecking and trampling order was quickly established. As soon as a parent bird alighted on the edge of the box, both necks extended upwards, straining and crying. But as they struggled, the larger bird more and more frequently pressed down on the other in order to stretch higher. Its creased and elderly-looking legs belied their dispassionate strength, the scrawny, elongated toes and their developing claws, gaining purchase wherever planted, on the body, neck or face of the other. And the parents continued to supply the most prominent beak.

After a week or so, the smaller chick, an albino

beautiful with all white feathers, was showing signs of weakening. It asserted itself less and less when a parent arrived, fell beneath the tread of the other more quickly, even looked as though its neck had less strength in the struggle for the food. I removed the larger one at times and held it in my hands, hoping the other would thrive if allowed occasional, exclusive access to its parents. But this made little difference. Sustenance of a more fundamental nature was missing. Each time the claws descended and its face was pushed down into the straw, each time both parents continued to disgorge the contents of their crops automatically into one beak but not the other, the hideous differences between the two chicks grew. I tried removing the albino and feeding it milk through a pipette from my chemistry set. Its neck and wings seemed slack and unable to compose themselves. It seemed reluctant to open its beak, it choked and was unable to retain much of the milk. Back in the nest box, there was no alteration of routine among any of the birds, no compensations, no recognition.

'It's dying'. 'It's had it, y' better ring its neck'. Other kids offered their advice, and I listened especially to those with older brothers whose worldliness I admired. 'Do you know how to?' 'It's dead easy'. 'Our Malcolm will do it if you can't'.

'All it needs is food, and not to be trodden on all the time'. I knew this but had been unable to have the slightest effect on the course of its decline. My parents did not know what to do either. I wanted to kill the bird myself, to do it swiftly and carefully, to be in contact with it when it died. The procedure had been explained to me, I held it as I would a larger bird, my forefinger behind the legs, the other three in front cradling the stomach and restraining it, my thumb across its back.

The small, slack body almost oozed between the gaps in my fingers. I knew what I had to do, place the first two fingers of my other hand either side of the neck then firmly and definitely, twist and pull at the same time. One turn, at least a quarter of the way around, further would be better. I felt its neck, the hopeless lack of strength, no sense of bone or structure for me to definitively crack and break. I was determined to be the executioner, to submit its body to one brief, last act of violence and free it from the daily round of humiliation and abandonment back in the loft.

Pull and turn; pull, twist and turn. I muttered the manoeuvres, holding the flaccid body and rehearsing. I was almost ready, one tiny instant away. Twist, snap, and pull, the baby bird's death groan, a saddened gargle of bubbles in the throat or a frantic final wheeze of breath. Twist and pull.

What if I failed, made half a move and then panicked, desperate to repair the destruction? What if I did all I was supposed to do, and it still didn't die but instead the neck, more hopeless still, just dangled further down the body? I couldn't do it. Pull, snap, done. I could not carry out this one quick, efficient act and become grown up - decisive and compassionate and unafraid.

My friend said his father, who kept pigeons himself, would do it that evening when he came home from work. I made further futile attempts with the pipette and it was still alive as I walked up later, alert to the rows of vegetables in the back gardens and a radio letting slip a pop song through an open window. I handed over the box feeling abject and not able to say much. He saw it in me and said 'Leave it with me, son. I'll take care of it when I've had my tea'.

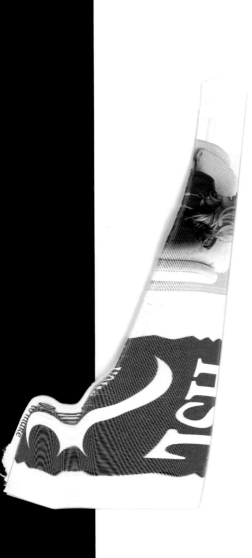

The Naples of England

The people of Weymouth, attentive to the horizon like predators weakened through a long winter, would muster their depleted energies during the first stirrings of Spring.

'They'll be flocking in if this weather keeps up'.

Shutters and awnings rattling, dust beaten out, accumulated pockets of sand swept from doorways, council vehicles parked up on the empty, pedestrians-only promenade. The clatter from lorry loads of deckchairs out of winter storage and being built into stacks on the beach. Canoes nestling like sardines. Huge floating craft across the backs of youths, their arms splayed as if in crucifixion, carried down to the water's edge. Narrow strutted jetties wheeled into the sea, prodding the retreating nip of winter still residing in the sea's temperature.

In the clear, exacting focus of a new season's light, beach stalls creaking open, crockery clinking and cups chattering in wire trays, urns subjected to trial runs with bulky masses of steaming water, serving hatches prising open, chalkboards brought out into the daylight, rows of hooks weighted down with joyous trivia. From rooftops, balconies and empty, stale interiors, the broken orchestration of hammer and saw, fresh resin and the heady musk of tar and paint. All in preparation for the silver shoals, the flocks alighting, the herds stopping to graze. Survival and restoration, appetite and livelihood.

My father would be out shopping in the town centre on summer Saturday mornings as early as he could.

'If you're not done and home before ten, you might as well forget it,' he would say.

We took in summer visitors, factory workers and their

families from the West Midlands, women and children from South Wales with their huge men who hewed the coal there. 'As long as they don't start singing,' my father once said, never completely happy with the opening up of our house in this way. My mother advertised in Daltons Weekly and selected regional newspapers. A neighbour had inducted her into the procedures but she secreted away what she believed to be the winning words with which she had constructed her three-line classified advertisement. This was the only way we could afford a holiday, my mother said, 'working my ruddy fingers to the bone,' fried breakfasts every morning carried on a tray into our best front room, sleeping arrangements in weekly flux, my box room the first to be requisitioned. Once I shared the pull-out sofa bed with my mother for the only time it was ever used. And on another occasion my father and I were in the kitchen on camp beds that had to be dismantled and packed away by 7.15 ready for him to shave at the sink and then for her to scramble pots and utensils ready for the daily conflagration of bacon, eggs, tomatoes and sausages.

Sometimes families were split between neighbouring houses, pot luck holidaying among the empty or vacated rooms along Purbeck Road. Others occasionally arrived unannounced, on the off chance. Their cases would be brought discretely inside our privet hedge and the people left standing in the garden, while my mother worked her way along the neighbouring doors, permutations being reckoned and resolved in the emergency negotiations. Sometimes there seemed to be transfers after dark, movement between safe houses. And whoever was found a bed, whatever their pairings or combinations, they were to be without trace on

Tuesday mornings when the council rent collector made his rounds, for fear that he might note any tell-tale irregularities, clues to contravention of our tenancy agreements.

As a child the physical appearance on maps of my home town and its surrounding coastline gave me a thrill each time I saw it. The Naples of England. That was what people called Weymouth, my father told me, because of its perfect bay. I took pride and pleasure in this.

Our town was situated at the meeting point of two huge tracts of water that curved in from opposite directions. To the east, the direction that our seafront hotels and esplanade faced, was Weymouth Bay, a perfect arc of golden sand leading first northwards and then round towards deserted, inaccessible cliffs and headlands that on fine days – and most were fine days - we could make out dipping and rising all the way to exotic destinations such as Durdle Door and Lulworth Cove. At the southern end of the town's beach, where the gently shelving sands dipped into a sea that seemed especially warmed in the bowl of the bay, was the Pleasure Pier which formed one of the two arms protecting the entrance to Weymouth Harbour.

And in the harbour, the ferry boats, passengers embarking to the Channel Islands, huge crates of tomatoes obscuring the sun as they were swung by cranes from the decks of cargo ships down towards us watchers on the dock. On still summer nights lying in bed a mile away in Purbeck Road I could hear the boat train clanking along tracks down the centre of Commercial Road carrying its passengers from the railway station to the waterside or screeching and grinding to a halt at some obstruction. If they passed us during the day, stopping the traffic, we could look up at the people in the carriage windows, sitting self-consciously looking down at us. With us but not of us, like the thousands who covered our sands at the height of the season.

Across the harbour, towering above the Stone Pier, was the Nothe Fort. From the ornamental gardens beside the fort, one could look in one direction down into the harbour and on towards the Pleasure Pier, sands and seafront. In the opposite direction was Portland harbour, battle grey ships, breakwaters with tiny lighthouse buoys, gates and railings and padlocks, access restricted to naval personnel, and then, throwing it all into scale, the huge bulk of Portland squatting in the sea some five miles away.

Along the Pleasure Pier, a huge platform with pontoons sunk into a dark and sunless sea, holidaymakers paraded in their numbers. My parents had met in their youth through the Swimming Club out at the end of this pier. I could just pick them out among the smiling young people, some tentative, others more defiant and self-assured, staring out from the old photograph. Ignore the hair styles and bathing caps, the one piece costumes. Ignore a war looming across Europe, and those faces in the strong summer sunshine could be looking out from the 1960s.

As the sands curled around to meet the Pleasure Pier, about a quarter of a mile from the Nothe gardens, there were the donkeys. When I was young, there was no greater treat than to ride in procession down the sea's edge on one of their backs. The warm, sweet smell from the dung dropped outrageously onto the sand, the creak and resinous scent from the saddle as I shifted position, the hardened bony back beneath the sparse wiry hair, all gave rare textures to being alive.

Right beside the donkeys, the sand modeller's enclosure, Frank Dinnington sculpting huge versions of Salisbury Cathedral, every transept, spire and window precisely fashioned. Or, the tableaux of the Last Supper, Jesus and the disciples, rounded shoulders and compassionate foreheads, their bodies leaning in towards each other. 'All made entirely from local sand and water,' said the scrawl on the board, and the pennies, threepenny and sixpenny bits trickled down from the promenade into the collecting buckets. Every so often, regularly it seemed, the local paper would carry a photograph of a collapsed cathedral wing, a mighty structure reduced to sand, and a story headlined something like 'Smashed by vandals'. And the coins would flow in a heavy torrent.

A further one hundred yards or so along the sands, you would reach the First Aid and the Lost Children's huts, a pair of semi-detached white painted wooden huts with an enclosure formed by a white picket fence. These dispensed disinfectant, ointments and a sense of protection.

Most summers we holidayed at home, or rather my brother and I ran full bodied between the thousands grouped in deckchair communities, squeezing between their encampments, in and out of the warm shallows, a whip of bladder wrack, if one could be found, lassoing the air.

'Be careful what you're doing with that around people's faces,' my mother might warn.

'Look out for that yellow dinghy,' or something similar she would explain so that we could eventually find our way back to her deck chair. 'And if all else fails go to the Lost Children's Hut'.

Another visitor attraction - why would we ever want to travel any further into England? – was the tall thin box painted in red, white and pale blue stripes, Frank Edmunds' Punch and Judy stall. Taking my penny for the collecting box as often as I could afford, I would ease my way in amongst all the visiting children who chanted when required or instructed. Singing through reeds or his huge curving nose, mad-eyed Mr Punch, with his stick to his shoulder, surveyed all below him seeing with a long, lingering look into each of our deceitful hearts.

'Judy, where's the baby?'

'Downstairs'

'Bring it up, bring it up'.

'OK, here's the baby'.

Thwack, thwack, thwack.

'That's the way to treat the old lady'.

One set of guests registered more than most with me when I was nine years old. A young couple, Paul and his fiancé, Marion, stayed one summer with his parents, occupying all three of our bedrooms A red haired, tubby and boundlessly enthusiastic young man, Paul asked my parents if I could accompany Marion and him on a fishing trip so that they could benefit from my knowledge of the choice locations. They also took me with them to the Fair. As much as the fishing, the Fair, the ice creams and the candy floss, I especially enjoyed evenings in our front room, which my parents had designated the 'visitors' lounge'. Just the three of us, Paul, Marion and myself while his parents went out, with me enlivening their stay with animated tales of local life.

'You can't keep going in that front room,' my mother said, oblivious to the camaraderie we shared. 'They've got to be allowed to have a bit of time to themselves'.

The next spring I was delighted when Paul wrote to my mother asking if they could again book a week's stay in August. But her manner clearly showed that she did not share my sense of joy.

'That Paul from Wolverhampton wants to come again, in August, peak season, with that fiancée of his,' my mother told my father when he arrived home from work that evening. 'Just the two of them'.

'Great!' I replied before my father could answer. 'They can, can't they?'

My mother waved the letter in an erratic fashion as if she was trying to shake it from her own grip.

'Says they just want the one room,' she added.

'I told you this sort of thing would happen when you started all this,' my father snapped. 'You'll have to write and tell them you're fully booked.'

'But we're not,' I said. 'Mum said so.'

My mother held my father's gaze, ignoring me.

'But why can't they come?' I persisted.

'They can't and that's that!'

'But why?' I asked one more time although I knew that by now the outcome was firmly settled.

Like Survivors

Ricky was particularly excited about the guns. The rifles. Not any old air rifles like the older kids around here had or the ones on the stall at the Fair, but proper weapons. He had seen them lined up in the cadet store with their polished butts and greased loading mechanisms, ready for use. He'd be allowed to handle them, begin his proper training, when he was fourteen. By his next birthday but one!

Ricky had changed a lot in the year he had been away. Although he had never been any taller than me, he now seemed to hold his shoulders further back, to push his nose and chin forward like an athlete perpetually reaching for a finishing tape. His freckles had subsided somehow and his hair was much tidier, cut in a way my Dad would have described as a good old-fashioned short back and sides. His face was thinner, more pointed, and I wondered whether he had been eating far fewer sweets and biscuits than the rest of us.

The cadets were the best bit of where he lived now, he told me. You went on manoeuvres, learned about discipline and had to dig your own hole to go to the toilet when you were camped out in the hills. At the end of the day when the tents were erected you could play British Bulldog. You had to learn how to look after yourself, he said, to find out who your mates were. It could turn into quite a scrap and get serious. You could get badly hurt if you didn't watch your back.

I had suggested that, as he was only visiting for a few days, we hang around up at The Rec like we used to do. But he hadn't wanted to meet up with our old gang. His flattened tone of voice and concentrated stare let me know clearly enough that he considered himself now far removed from those childish past times.

'We should have an adventure. Like commandoes,' he said. 'Get ourselves lost and have to find our way back'.

And so I foolishly let slip the secret I had been entrusted with, that one of the kids last week had heard the booming of a bittern out in the Reed Beds. That there might be a nest.

His indifference vanished. An excitement flushed through him, widening his gaze and sharpening his posture as if he were detecting a scent.

'Let's hunt it down,' he said, 'like we're survivors or something'.

*

Ricky had lived on Mendip Street, less than ten minutes' walk from me, and I played there once or twice. His older sister Miriam was more dramatically freckled, the colour of her thick red hair splattered also across her face and arms. She sat at the dining table, in her school uniform, her books covered in flowery wallpaper and piled amongst the tea things. Sometimes Ricky and I made plans for a den in their shed. I encouraged him to seek approval for our plans from his mother, he invented excuses not to do so.

'She had a ruddy cheek, if you ask me,' my mother said of his. 'She just dumped him off in the school holidays with his slippers one day, first thing in the morning. Said he had to be home by half past five. Never asked me, just assumed I'd give him his dinner. And his tea, probably. Of course I would, but the cheek of it. Just dropped him off like that, first thing in the morning, with his slippers, expected me to look after him all day.'

One Saturday afternoon, some months before he left Mendip Street, we played at my house with my old clockwork train set, a figure of eight track with an infinity of possibilities. When the engine slowed and stopped, we inserted the key and rewound the spring as close to its coiled limit as it would take. But the game ground to a halt when the key became mislaid. We looked everywhere, underneath and behind the chairs and settee, my parents joining in as my patience collapsed into a noisy despondency.

'Try to think where you last saw it. Did you come into the kitchen with it at all?'

We searched down the backs of cushions, in the drawers of cupboards, in increasingly improbable locations. The game was over and my parents advised that we found something else to play and that it would turn up. There was no substitute though to the urgent fantasies that we had built alongside the tracks and the mood deflated into a long wait until teatime.

Some while later, as we failed to find any game that could begin to match the one that had been denied us, my father came into the room and said

'Ricky, I want you to have a good look in your pockets and see if there is anything in there that shouldn't be there'.

Ricky fumbled with his hankie, jiggling both hands emphatically up and down in his pockets.

'Have a good look,' my father said, and Ricky pulled out the key.

'I must have put it in by mistake,' he said gloomily.

Later when he had gone home, I asked my father how he had guessed. He suspected something, he said, when Ricky had gone to the toilet and he had heard a metallic object drop to the floor.

My father had once again brought resolution to the seemingly insoluble, just as when he succeeded with cryptic crossword clues in his newspaper or showed me a short cut for multiplying by eleven.

'But then he must have known where it was all that time we were searching,' I puzzled.

I had to accept that Ricky must have engaged me in a convincing deception but his motivation for doing so eluded and bothered me.

'He didn't want you to enjoy yourself, that's why,' my father explained. 'He's just spiteful'.

More shocks were to come a few months later though.

'I'm leaving in a couple of weeks' he told me.

I couldn't grasp his meaning. Leaving what? Our gang at The Rec?

'I'm going to Barnardo's, in South Wales'.

That was miles away, hundreds of miles, another country.

Nobody I knew had ever moved away. Our great post-War cohort of children had pushed forward together on a common front, dividing only at the great schism that followed the 'eleven plus'.

'What do you mean, Barnardo's?'

I had heard the word somewhere, it had connotations of sadness. It was nothing to do with us.

'For a holiday or something?'

And when he did move, I puzzled in front of my mother about the reasons for his departure. Ricky had told me how exciting it would be, there would be lots of activities he said, and he made it sound as though there would probably be no school.

'It was the mother - and that Grann,y' my mother explained. 'They drove the father out first. He had to go and live on Cumberland Road on his own. But he was a nice man, the dad. A bit soft but he always spoke to me. They kept the daughter though, she was useful. A girl, see. She could help in the house When they'd got rid of the dad, then it was Ricky's turn. He was a bit of a little monkey, mind you. There was that business with the key for your train set. He had it in his pocket all along. They probably thought he was going to be a handful so they got rid of him. They sent him to Barnardo's. All that way away and he was only a little nipper. It's supposed to be for orphans, for poor little beggars who've got no mothers or fathers. But they just sent him off anyway'.

My mother returned many times to the subject of Ricky and the cold-hearted expulsion from his family, always prefacing her remarks with 'Do you remember that Ricky? They lived down Pennine Road'.

Of course I remembered Ricky, and his walking away. It was an August evening in the dying light of a high summer day and a spectacular parachute practice filled the sky. A bulbous barrage balloon anchored up in the sunset, streams of tiny figures slipping away from the underside, like elvers on the current, tiny mushrooms sprouting and bobbing, and then the slow, swaying descent to the airfield far away behind rows and rows of houses.

We were up at the Rec, children everywhere, the noisy and dominant commandeering the big rocking gondola and taking it to its limits through sickeningly larger arcs. The little kids who had climbed aboard at the beginning were unable now to escape and clung to the worn iron handles, sweating it out. Elsewhere, on the individual swings, smaller groups of twos and threes dawdled or worked the seats and chains round and round into tightening spirals. Shouts, screams and threats bounced from the backs of the houses that bordered the three sides of the field.

I absorbed the energy from all around me, as I always did, aware that it was Ricky's last night with us. He was leaving in the morning on a train, on a journey beyond mine or anybody else's imagining.

But I could forget all that, or put it well to one side, among the gangs running and whooping through the grass and the crank and groan of the huge, green, metallic monster now again ascending slowly and rhythmically towards its mighty zenith.

'I've got to go now,' he said, turning to me. Some of the others knew too but he had spoken directly to me.

'Yeah. Well, I'm allowed to stay out for another half an hour'.

He continued to look at me.

'I'm going in the morning'.

The parachutes had ceased, the sun inched further behind the houses and the barrage balloon was being cranked slowly and invisibly back down to earth

'Yeah. But you're gonna visit your mum, aren't you?'

'Next year'.

'Yeah'

And he turned and began to walk away. I felt foolish, aware of the others around me, just standing watching him wading through the long grass in his short trousers, as if in a stream, towards the exit and out onto the road. He did not turn to look back at us even though I expected him to, and I was aware that many had stopped their games and conversations also to stare at Ricky on his long walk. The roaring had dimmed, the evening focused our muddled comprehension.

'Good riddance!' shouted Carol Devaney, puncturing the solemnity. And some of the others laughed and jeered.

He must have heard. He didn't flinch, yet alone turn. But he must have been able to tell that it was a girl's cry. She was standing right behind me, but he must have known it wasn't me. If he had turned, I would have waved, shown some expression of good will, but he disappeared out into the road without looking back, locking our history and our parting into himself.

*

A bittern out in the Reed Beds!

This wide expanse lay far beyond parental oversight and jurisdiction. From the furthest end of the Sports Field, an exit through a brambled gap in the hedge and a steep descent of Slippery Slope led to its perimeter. Various openings between the tall grasses, reeds and rushes allowed access to a network of trails too complex to memorise. Twisting a way through clearings and intersections, burrowing deeply into an interior dry and dusty in places, waterlogged in others, I was always anxious that, unlike Theseus, I had no method or system of clues to help me find the route back out.

We had sticks. We always carried sticks.

'Get your rifle up!' Ricky commanded, raising both arms above his head, his stick held between them.

I lifted my arms and stick as instructed, feeling foolish and unable, unwilling, to extend them as rigidly, and in such a disciplined a manner, as Ricky.

We found a nest, a mallard's not the bittern's, just to the side of the track where it began to disappear beneath a layer of blackened water. We must have been somewhere near Chafey's Lake, perhaps on its western edge. There were upwards of a dozen mottled green eggs, almost two layers of them, surrounded by a loosely-woven ring of twigs as if arranged with care and an eye for composition.

'Get down! We stake this out until the parent birds return,' he said, holding out his hand behind him as a signal for me to halt and then dropping to a crouching stance. 'That's our dinner tonight sorted'.

But it was an impossible position to maintain, even for a few minutes. I had a sharp pain at the back of my knees straight away and a dull ache in my thighs. Water had seeped right through into my new basketball boots.

'They won't come back while you make that row,' he said although, in truth, his own wriggling was causing as much rustling and swaying of the undergrowth.

'Okay then,' he said, suddenly straightening back up. 'Let's see how they like this'.

He picked up one of the eggs, tossed it lightly in his palm and then threw it towards where he judged the lake to be, threw it with all the force he could muster. We heard it land with a dull plop and he grunted in solemn approval.

'Go on,' he said. 'Your turn'.

'Go on!' he said again more insistently as I hesitated.

Then he stepped forward and brought one foot down into the middle of the nest.

'Let's see how they like this!'

None of the eggs could have survived that impact. The nest itself was smashed into a ragged mess of individual twigs. But still he kept on stamping, the whole of his body weight behind each blow.

'Let's - see – how – you – like – that!'

Only a Book

'He's reading, Mr Miller. That's the main thing. It doesn't matter what it is, as long as he's reading'.

My father was reporting back from a visit to my primary school parents' evening, where he had expressed a concern about my fondness for comics. He enjoyed these occasions and gave detailed reports afterwards about each line of the conversation as well as the reasoning behind each of his questions. He was clearly keen to be perceived as a conscientious and interested parent and I appreciated that. But I also experienced other feelings that seemed more resentful and unworthy on my part, something about his own need for approval from teachers with me being merely the pretext.

Thankfully, my teacher had supported my current reading preferences.

My father also referred to 'the classics' frequently although on our regular visits to the public library, he always returned with crime novels for my mother and himself. I meanwhile made a steady progression from Enid Blyton through Richmael Crompton to Capt. W.E. Johns. Much though I loved the serious bulk, the embossed covers and the gauge of the paper in the occasional hardback books bought for me as Christmas presents by kindly relatives, the *Swiss Family Robinson* and *Lorna Doone* remained unread on our sideboard, receiving little from me by way of serious study.

When I was ten we went as a family to London. My Dad secreted some of our holiday money in each of his shoes and I mused on the likely identifying features of pick pockets. Arriving in the immensity of Waterloo Station, we crossed the road outside, negotiating more traffic than I had ever seen, and entered the Union Jack Club.

Then in the following week we took in the vastness of the city - Madame Tussauds, the Natural History Museum, the Planetarium and, to my great delight, the second hand bookshops along Charing Cross Road. There I found an Agatha Christie that I had not read, the one about the ten people on an island who are all murdered one by one. When we took a boat trip down the Thames from Tower Bridge to Greenwich that afternoon, I sat up on deck reading this book and missed all the sights.

'Had his nose in that book the whole way,' my father later remarked.

So it was a relief all round when, in my second year at the grammar school, the set book in English turned out to be *Moonfleet* by J Meade Faulkner. A relief because, to my Dad the book had an obvious aura of serious literary merit and because the village of Fleet was only half a dozen miles or so from where we lived.

'We used to have a member of our family kept the key for Fleet Church,' my father told me, prompting me to make a cycle trip there.

At the churchyard, I could not bring myself to step onto the heaped mounds even though I very much wished to relive the terror that Jim Trenchard had experienced in the book. Although I had seen nobody as I freewheeled down through the village, I was nonetheless very aware of the deep disrespect that would be conveyed if I were to stand on top of the graves. Just looking from the edge though I could imagine the rumbling of the contraband barrels eddying in the vaults below. I was still able with Jim to mistake their crashing for the groans and disquiet of the dead.

The track from the church soon petered out at the edge of a salt water lagoon, The Fleet, a narrow stretch of water nipped between Chesil Beach and a scruffy, little-visited stretch of the mainland. Although it looked tranquil - brackish almost – much of the Fleet's eight miles of water disgorged and then replenished itself on the tide each day at Ferrybridge through a tiny access channel.

'You wouldn't think it but there's a vicious current runs through there,' my Dad explained. 'The whole Fleet is a danger trap. It's only half a mile or so wide at the most and seems so calm. You get a false sense of security'.

'So why is it so dangerous then?' I asked.

'It's the mud. It's not very deep, see, at low tide and you get stuck. You think you can walk and then the tide starts. You find out you can't swim and you can't walk. That's how it gets you once you're stuck'.

I knew this was no story exaggerated by my father for dramatic effect. We had the proof in our under stairs cupboard in the shape of a beautiful, adult-sized fishing rod that I was given by my father to share with my brother. He was reluctant to say more about its origins but the story did eventually come out – three men from his works, fishing from a boat in the Fleet at night, the water seemingly little more than inches deep, one of the widows wanting the rod to go to my Dad's boys.

When we finally finished reading *Moonfleet* in class some months later, I asked whether my Dad would take me to Portland so that I could look out into the vastness of West Bay and see for myself the setting for the book's dramatic conclusion.

'They call it the Isle of Portland,' my father explained although my brother and I had both heard this explanation many times before. 'But really it's an isthmus,' he added as the three of us made the train journey on a Sunday afternoon in February.

An isthmus, as the map so clearly revealed. Where Chesil Beach, the road and railway all fused together at their southern end there was Portland, the huge, obstinate snout of limestone wedged immovably among the tides and turmoil of the English Channel like a heavy, broken pendulum. Sitting high on the sea, some five miles in length, home to both a borstal and a prison, it was another country, a giddy, foreign excursion so potentially close at hand.

This landscape was a whole world, varied enough to offer adventure, mystery and horror. Cut off and protected, it seemed, from all the concerns that sullied national newspaper headlines it was nonetheless accorded recognition and a special place by the rest of the world in the nightly tolling from London for those in peril on the sea.

'… Dogger … Finistere … Portland Bill …'

There were few people in the streets when we disembarked and even fewer as we left the pavement at a place where pebbles had spilled into the road. As we climbed the embankment, our feet slurred across the smaller shingle but steadied in the larger stones with a clink or scrape of realignment. When we reached the crest the wind picked up from the sea blowing an insolent spray into our faces.

From the top we could see below us the monstrous and unsettled water. The winter slipped a degree or two towards its malignant heart. The wind broke in various directions, picking at our clothes and hair, making wet flecks. The grey sky eased further from its zenith and the activity of the sea increased in its restless, caged persistence.

'Do you want to go down a bit?' Dad asked.

The bank dropped steeply before levelling, rising slightly over a subsidiary scarp and then falling directly into the foam and oblivion. To the north, as far as the visibility would allow, I could see this huge geometry elongated. Dad told us that sailors and fishermen, if they were washed ashore on the beach at night or in a storm, could tell where they were from the size of the pebbles, large stones here at the Portland end diminishing along a very fine gradient to grit and then sand some eighteen miles away near Bridport. With thrilling ingenuity they could therefore judge in which direction to trudge the soonest to meet dry, level and unshifting land.

I found my father's hand, cold without a glove. 'Can we just go down to that bit?' I asked.

Descending to the dip, the larger stones creaking and groaning but staying in place, we met the sea in its own domain. Some thirty or forty yards out, the surface waters, already treading horrifying depths, paced about as if in agitation. Slowly a firmer constitution formed, a smoother, more coherent body, swelling and rearing, as if to claim the sky itself. Then the huge wave rushed in towards us, seeming unstoppable but tripping on itself some fifteen feet before the shore, breaking and convulsing onto the huge sloping platform of battered pebbles. Gulls wheeled away, their terror inaudible. A furious rush of foam and water, a pounding on stone, the upward lick of the furthest froth thinning into weak, exhausted fingers still clawing upwards.

And then silence, the sea empty and spent before its three melancholy witnesses. Secure, unharmed, salt water full in our faces, I wanted to step further down to scorn the water's last vague trickle. Instead we aimed our stones at its splayed-out body, made our purposeless incisions.

'It's the undertow, see. Doesn't matter how hard you try to get out, you get pulled back in,' said Dad.

Late that night in bed I read again the final chapters of *Moonfleet*, the fate of Elzever Block engulfing me in the shadows of the sleeping house. This kindly pirate, rough-hewn protector to Jim, thrown from the shipwreck off Chesil Beach, thrashing in the foam among the splintered struts and mast of the ship, unable to maintain his footing in the undertow, weakening in his grip on the rope from the shore, taken back forever into the depths, the storm triumphing wet, dispassionate and cold.

Afterwards, I could not settle or sleep for my tears so I shuffled into my parents' bedroom, waking them, looking for some calm or even irritable voices to assuage me of the wicked wildness of the Bay.

'Whatever's the matter?' my mother mumbled, still half asleep, and I attempted to explain my upset through my embarrassment.

The dragging retreat. Pebbles, grasped by the sea, scraped together back down into the dark body of the water

'It's alright,' she said. 'Just go back to bed'.

The screeching stones building into a gigantic cry, the whole beach being torn from itself, being carried back to the cold foundries in which it was first forged.

'And try not to go waking your brother up,' my father added. 'After all, it's only a book'.

Mentors for the Atomic Age

My earliest years at school and the final one or two stood out as exciting excursions through a stunning landscape of human accomplishment and knowledge. The intervening decade or more, by contrast, seemed like an unending trudge through featureless marsh and scrub.

The greatest treat in my infant school years, for instance, took place at the end of the final year when I was seven. Our teacher, Miss Cartwright, took our whole class to Rossi's ice cream parlour all the way up on the seafront. Its dark, fan-cooled interior had always seemed the territory of the visiting holidaymaker. On that day though, an area at the back was cordoned off and reserved just for us. We still rushed between the other tables though to claim our seats as if they were rationed, the winner takes it all. Local children, we asserted our right to partake too of the banana split and the knickerbocker glory. The slower, the weaker and the more polite were pushed to the back or pulled from their seats. Miss Cartwright attempted to rein back the boisterous excesses with kind words and smiles, the wounded and the dispossessed congregating around her skirts, vying limply for a place at her table. I assumed Miss Cartwright's wealth to be substantial, she was paying for everybody and many attempted to seize huge chunks of her generosity for themselves.

'Can I have an American ice cream soda?' Karl Jospin yelled, trampling us with his worldliness.

And Miss Cartwright laid out other gifts before us through the year.

'What happens when you've done all the red books?' I once enquired.

'There are the brown ones'.

'And what's after that?'

'Then there are purple ones'.

'And what's after that?'

'Then you can choose from the library corner, anything you want. And in the summer, there will be a trip to the public library down by the harbour. You can become a member'.

'What's after subtraction?

'Then it's subtraction of hundreds, tens and units'.

'And what's after hundreds, is it called thousands?'

'After that we go on to something completely new'.

'What's that called?'

'It's called multiplication but you probably won't get there until next year'.

A waitress in a uniform brought a tray of fizzing drinks, orange and raspberry, some in bottles with straws, two straws to each bottle, and others in moulded glass tumblers. Cakes on a large plate were brought, one for each of us from a selection. Elizabeth White on my table grabbed for one of the two cream buns, 'I'm having that,' and then three of us lunged for the other. Karl Jospin won, stamping the back of my outstretched hand with his fist and pulling at the cardigan sleeve of my distant cousin, Janet.

'Look, I'm drunk,' shouted Elizabeth, her mouth full of cake and the bottle in her hand spilling, as she feigned an escalating wooziness.

'No, look, I'm drunk,' countered Karl and as he opened his mouth for a roar or an intoxicated dirge, a huge belch emerged instead. After the briefest flicker of panic, his bullfrog laugh became the loudest of all. And then he vomited. A forceful orange fountain splattered across the table and then, as he turned in disarray, a second less intense expulsion lodged itself in the coarse green weave of Elaine's cardigan sleeve, a chorus of disgust rising from our table, chairs kicked back in escape, an acrid odour, a sticky anxiety, the pollution of our feast.

Not all my teachers elicited the affection that Miss Cartwright so easily evoked although most provided a serviceable focus for my wandering imagination. My parents had no fond memories of their own schooling, my mother never mentioning any individuals by name as if for her they had all coalesced into one solid mass of authority to be resented and avoided. 'I had no concentration that was my problem. If somebody said I had to do something, then I didn't want to. Defiance it was, I suppose'. My father, on the hand, had their names – Bug Welford, old Freddie Babb - contempt or fear, I was never sure which, fuelling the listing of their nicknames. He had a line of whitened skin across the base of his right hand little finger, I used to see it and feel its ridge when my brother and I lay in bed with him some Sunday mornings when we were young, each of us working a hand and wrist as if a puppet, him doing the voices while my mother made cups of tea downstairs.

The scar was the result of a lifelong wound, well almost lifelong, inflicted by a teacher's cane when he was seven years old. On his first day at junior school, the deputy head had entered my father's classroom and fired arithmetical questions around the class. My father had mumbled a reply when his turn came, correctly but inaudibly, and was summoned to the front and instructed to extend his left hand.

The closest I came to such depravities, punishments that my father always seemed to judge as well deserved, was in my final year in the junior school. I had somehow been selected for Mr Stoddard's class, the eleven plus crammer. We'd been creamed off we were told, thirty nine of us, and we were to be pushed. Every day, whether sodden from a downpour on the walk to school on a gloomy, winter morning or enlivened by the spirit of a new spring filled with sunshine, we performed our lightning speed observances. Mental arithmetic, tables and addition and subtraction. The missing figure, the next in the sequence, the odd one out. And spellings, more and more spellings. Old Stoddard, lean, elderly and mean spirited, patrolled our cowering rows, beating out the pace, demanding participation. My back straightened, my arm jabbed upwards, my body was alert and twitching as if sensing a kill. All day it seemed we were drilled in these routines, all day except for the regular blocks of time when the others were in the playground and I was indoors under his peripheral view writing out lines, 'I must learn to behave myself in class,' 'I must concentrate and avoid silliness'. However many of these lines I accrued, all logged meticulously in Stoddard's punishment book in red ink, still more were showered upon me.

'It says 'Crude Oil Production' on this poster. Look, it says 'crude'. That's rude'.

'Miller! One hundred lines, I must learn to control myself in class. By Friday!'

Sometimes my backlog seemed to tower above me at an unstable height, my left-handed scrawl slowing to a crawl, completion and my eventual freedom seeming impossible. Once, seeing a new depth to my despair, my mother offered to produce some of the pages herself.

'Now, how do you want me to do these? she asked. 'I used to be in trouble at school, my Mum got proper cross with me if I took home a bad report. Don't tell your Dad I've helped you'.

Her rounded, flowery letters bore no resemblance to mine, the forgery would be apparent to all. It was an ill-crafted attempt and bound to fail.

'That's not right. It's too curvy. He'll see it straight away and know it's not me!'

I passed for the grammar school nevertheless and my world cleaved. New people, new buildings in a new area of the town, important-sounding subjects, room changes, and a heady swirl of laboratories and foreign languages. And for a while school felt more settled. I became purposeful, engaged and more anonymous. But within a couple of years, bottom of the top form in all my end of term exams, I was back to being academically ill-at-ease and regularly serving after school detentions on Thursday nights.

All my reports spoke of unfulfilled potential and a persisting immaturity. One evening in particular our whole class was kept in after school for some collective misdemeanor by a lanky and much ridiculed religious studies teacher. At twenty past four, most of the girls were allowed to leave while the rest of us continued to copy set passages from the Bible. Others who had settled to their task without wise-cracking were allowed to exit in dribs and drabs as the clock hands dragged silently through first five, then six and eventually seven o'clock. By that time only two of us were left bent over our pages and then Mr Chivers let the other boy leave. Suddenly feeling dry-mouthed and vulnerable, I suffered in an appalling silence sensing that some act of unspeakable indecency was about to befall me.

Mr Chivers walked down the aisle to my desk and then hoisted himself in his heavy jacket and trousers up onto the wonky individual desk in front of mine. He perched there precariously, the informality he seemed to be seeking so obviously eluding him, and then I sensed him bending down even closer to my bowed head.

'Miller ...' he began, with what seemed to me to be a ring of feigned affection. 'Miller, is there anything wrong at home?'

*

My father's belief in rationality and scientific advance was a matter of faith. 'You can't argue with progress, Andrew,' he often told me. And it was true that I did feel myself privileged to be living in modern times, standing with everybody else at the perimeter of the Atomic Age. Indeed, a little later, as sixth formers, my physics class was taken on a special visit to the nearby Winfrith nuclear power plant where we climbed the short iron ladder and stood in our school uniforms on top of the reactor. I bent to touch its roughened surface, the few feet of warm and vibrating concrete beneath our feet that separated us from a caged, minor sun struggling to burst out into the universe.

The bright beacons of education would lead us all out from the evils borne of ignorance. It would have spared my parents and the whole adult world the Dark Age they had had to live through. And yet the agents of this enlightenment - old Stoddard, Mr Chivers and all the rest of them – seemed to me remarkably ill cast for the heroic duties that history was forcing onto them.

Miss Cartwright had shown us affection but we had been very young then. The first teacher who seemed to me to be in step with the urgency of the times was Irene Fletcher, the biology teacher at my grammar school whom I first met when I was thirteen through membership of the Field Club. This club focused ostensibly on the natural world and landscape and met after school in the biology lab as well as for weekend walks in the surrounding countryside. Most members were a few years older than my friend, Paul, and I but we were tolerated as we joined them at benches on high stools, surrounded by glass fronted cupboards containing rows of old stained jars inside of which organic entities pickled away. The discussions sported a high degree of play acting and histrionics as we considered matters as diverse as art, aesthetics, theology and literature, the energetically-suppressed courtship of some of the older ones being an embarrassment we feigned not to notice as the price of our inclusion.

Irene was treasured by the older pupils as a confidante, an advisor, and a safe refuge from the prim anonymity of their early 1960s home lives. On first name terms outside of school, she dressed on walks in a white fisherman's jumper and blue denim jeans, clashing with all my previous experience of teachers. Some of the older pupils had been known to walk from Weymouth the whole five miles out along the beach road to her cottage on Portland, to share with her their struggles for identity, to seek counsel over parents, or to share with her their latest creation - a sketch, painting or poem.

After a year or so of membership, there was the sensational announcement of a Field Club party to be held at Irene's cottage on a Saturday evening. At fourteen, the last party I had attended would have been my own birthday six or seven years earlier when Brian Roberts had ripped his best grey flannel jacket on barbed wire on the way. My mother, equally or more distressed, spent much of the event attempting to effect an invisible mend in the heavy material. Clearing the debris afterwards, we both knew, and with some relief, that this would be the last one. Enough of the sweat and bruises, the acid regurgitation and the wild urination.

But a party at a teacher's house! My parents fussed over the clothes I should wear, were insistent on my showing respect, remembering my manners and being polite. 'It's not that sort of a party,' I snapped but I was really as anxious as they were, none of us having any template for the life lived beyond this social threshold.

'Just remember to do what you're told, if anybody asks you'.

'Dad! '

'Well, nobody ever got anywhere, you know, by proving the boss wrong'.

Irene's cottage was a battered, pink-washed, double fronted building. I was welcomed into her softly-lit living room where a type of music I had never heard before, a lazy saxophone wandering around a brushed snare drum, was playing. Her chairs were much smaller than ours and made of unvarnished wood, there was no linoleum on the floor just mats on top of bare stone. There were paintings on the walls, real ones, nudes even and melancholy figures, some of them vaguely familiar. The older pupils stood in the centre of the room talking loudly and sipping drinks. A few of the boys were wearing cravats beneath open-necked shirts and some of the girls, in what seemed an absurd attempt to mimic grown women, were wearing nylons and smeared make-up. Irene offered me a glass of brown ale, only my second ever alcoholic drink. I struggled to understand the conversation of the older pupils and certainly could offer no contribution.

Feeling tense and alert, swimming in the malty tang of my drink, the rows of books provided a secure fix for my attention. In our living room at home, we had a bible, an old encyclopedia, a digested compendium of Dickens, and I curated my own slim collection of Enid

Blyton, Just William and Biggles books. On Irene's shelves, however, were rows and rows of books with green or orange spines, paperbacks, their titles provocative and sophisticated. I scanned them with my head tilted to one side as the effects of the brown ale pulled me further over and down towards the floor - *'The L-Shaped Room,' 'Vile Bodies,' 'The Heart Is A Lonely...'*

'Everybody, everybody. Here's a challenge, a competition. You have to find the roundest pebble on the beach you can. The winner is the most aesthetically pleasing curvature, the smoothest pebble. Don't get lost!'

Outside in the blind night, zig-zagging winds buffeted the worn edges of the last line of buildings before the shingle bank. Here was a challenge I could meet. I pulled at rocks embedded in the ground, tears of excitement blurring my vision as I palmed their chilled surfaces.

My life of running, the hiding and the seeking, now entering a world of new and expanding possibilities. Indefinite tracks leading off into the future, journeys hinted at with only the briefest of directions, journeys that I could not and would not refuse to undertake.

The heart indeed a lonely hunter.

Racing Right Away

In 1963, I obtained a summer job in one of the arcades on the seafront collecting money on the bingo stall owned and operated by Jack and Mary West. I stood with Mary inside, collecting the sixpenny stakes from the double rows of plastic seats that surrounded us on three sides. Jack sat on a swivel chair on a raised platform, hunched behind his machine bubbling with coloured and numbered ping pong balls, microphone in one hand, cigarette in the other, weariness sagging through his frame.

'Come on in, we're racing right away. Come on in'.

Circumspect, regular with my weekly wages, these two had somehow ended up in the artificial light of an amusement arcade on a Dorset seafront. But, Mary told me, in their younger days they had travelled the world in a South African circus, turning their hands to whatever was required with Jack even facing the lions in their cage. 'Show him what they did,' she one day said to Jack and, after further cajoling from her, he reluctantly raised the back of his shirt – great angry swipes across the whole of his back, permanent registrations carried across continents.

'Eyes down, looking in'.

The outside world pulsed through the gossip of the regular players. The majority of the clientele were predictably regular, a tightly defined and almost entirely female demographic. Buzzing between them collecting their dues, I could pick up the latest snippets and titbits from the Profumo affair. I had carefully torn black and white photos of Christine Keeler and Mandy Rice-Davies from my father's Daily Express at home and stashed them away. It was unbelievable to me that women so shamefully desirable, grown women not girls, actually existed somewhere. My mother must have found and disposed of them because they always disappeared.

But the whispers on the bingo stall were as much, or more, concerned with the trial of the osteopath, Stephen Ward. I looked up the word 'osteopath' in a dictionary but the prosaic, paramedical definition gave no clue to the real substance behind the frisson that this seemed to generate both in newspaper accounts and among the clucking rows of bingo players. And then one day, raised excitement rippled around the two rows, shocked gasps, greedy whispering, back and forth – Stephen Ward had committed suicide! First, John F Kennedy and now this.

Christine Keeler, Mandy Rice-Davies and the McGregor sisters, Carol and Mary, who lived two streets away from me on Bodmin Road. A rumour went around the kids up at the Rec one night when I was about fifteen

'Mary McGregor was down the Sports Field without her clothes on last night. Anyone could have a feel. They say she's going down again tonight'.

I could barely raise my voice loud enough to ask Alan Avery whether this was really true.

'Straight up,' he said. 'Our Jimmy was there, said you could see everything'.

Even more weakly now, ashamed of my need for the information, I asked him if he knew at what time.

Mr McGregor was in prison according to my father but he would not say what for. I was, however, able to obtain from him enough by way of reassurance that it was for not for murder or violent, armed robbery. Intrigued as well as unsettled to be living so close to a professional class criminal, I was warned away by my father.

'A nasty piece of work and no mistake. Prison's the best place for him'.

As a child I believed that my parents could name every person resident in Weymouth, that they could tease out the links between an entire population, knit together every loose scrap of knowledge, each acquaintance and relation. And it had become clear that in this web were shared understandings, somehow operating at a level inaccessible to me, of crimes pushed deeply beneath the daily discourse of the town. Hidden and unspoken too were the true activities of osteopaths.

Karl Jospin and Carol McGregor stood near the entrance to the Field that night and watched me closely while I avoided their eyes. I had barely seen either of them in seven or eight years, our destinies after infant school having been determined first by junior school catchment areas that carved up our estate and then by the 'eleven plus' which sealed their lifelong separation.

There was a busy mass of bending figures discernible in the half light up by the further goal posts as I passed Karl and Carol with my head bent towards the ground. They looked at me in silence, neither smirking nor calling out. Feeling wretched and exposed, I tried and failed to concoct at least for myself the deception of some other purpose or destination.

At the scrum, I recognised some of the fat-thighed boys who were pushing and snorting as coming from our estate. But there were also strangers who must have travelled from other parts of the town. My heartbeat and shivering limbs settled a little when I realised that there was nobody else from the grammar school. With individuals curiously anonymous and unspeaking, I grappled to extend a hand between the bodies and into the centre of the circle, to reach and touch flesh and resolve the mystery, to subdue the insistent pull into shame and misery. Dropping to my knees, I could see between their legs a figure on the ground, presumably Mary McGregor, and extend my hand to touch something human, maybe her arm or perhaps her thigh. It was not her breast, I was fairly sure, but the indiscriminate jostling threatened too many blows and bruises if I persisted in my grim desire. Somebody said that Karl Jospin had Durex and I felt even more sickened.

Down at the entrance to the Field, Karl and Carol were standing side by side in the twilight facing two older youths whom I did not recognise. There was something passed between them, the sense of a negotiation, a compromise or a surrender.

I next saw Carol McGregor about a year later up on the promenade in the furnace heat and bustle of a midsummer's day. Arm and arm with a lad a little older than me, not somebody I had ever noticed before, they strode together like a couple on a poster advertising escape and fulfilment in their little seaside resort. Wholesome in her billowing dress, full-hearted roses on cream, held in at the waist by a large white belt, her happiness was impossible to hide. Although she had been one of the less pretty of my infant school companions, her smile that afternoon, more than her permed brown hair and the make-up, propelled her into the sunlight, a world away from the degradation that had dried up my mouth that evening down at the Field.

I watched them walk all the way to the Jubilee Clock, feeling lighter myself, as they reached around each other's waists, then resumed their linking of arms, before crossing the road and disappearing towards the side streets down by the station. The sauntering crowds swallowed up their absence and the afternoon heat built further, the wind off the sea carrying children's cries of laughter and protest, fragments of Mr Punch's menacing whine, the intermittent clack of deckchairs on their stack and the toffee-like aroma of donkey droppings.

And then that same afternoon, only an hour or so later and before the teatime thinning of the crowds, I saw her again. Among the promenading couples and families, the small children scraping metal spades along the esplanade and the teenagers sitting in a row along the railings, Carol was walking again in an excited embrace but this time with a sailor in full uniform. His bell-bottomed trousers were flapping as they crossed the road, leaving the open air, holiday bustle and disappearing down those very same side streets.

Come on in, we're racing right away.

Fifty Miles is a Long Way

'Let the word go forth from this time and place ... '
President Kennedy's rhetoric had held my attention
and fired my ambition in a way that the crusty and
pompous tones of our own country's great and good
never would.

' ... the torch has been passed to a new generation.'
If the American marines had been only half-hearted
about accepting their president's challenge to walk fifty
miles in a day then the young people of Britain would
show that we were up to it and would step forward.

A friendly rivalry between the two countries and a
way of honouring their assassinated president was how
Gopher had put it in morning assembly. And a chance to
prove what we were capable of. It would reflect well on
the school he said, show the 'character' of its pupils. And
now there was the possibility that the event might even
feature on the television, on South Today.

'That's the only reason you're doing it,' said Dick. 'So
you can be on the telly'.

I protested. The immensity of the challenge had
impressed me straight away. The outrageous notion of
walking fifty miles had been conceived far away from
the parochial concerns of our provincial grammar
school.

'You were just the same,' sneered Dick, 'when you
went in that marathon twist competition up on the
esplanade last year and they only ended up showing a
couple of seconds on the local news'.

Although Dick was probably right, I did not want to
concede the point publicly and lose face in front of our
friends. And it was true that I had secretly hoped the
camera would single me out dancing furiously to

Chubby Checker. But I had been younger then, a whole year younger.

Only Terry and Dick were showing any enthusiasm for the walk. The others - Paul, Ernie and Simon - exempted themselves with various lame excuses.

'There was that doctor woman, what was it, Dr Barbara Moore?' said Ernie. 'Always on the news. Walking from Lands End to John O'Groats'.

'A nutcase,' added Paul. 'Called herself a vegetarian. Didn't eat meat.'

'No protein' said Dick. 'Sheer folly. Essential for body strength.'

We were all sitting in the long lounge of Dick's parents' bungalow out along the beach road, drinking coffee. His father, Mr Towers, was the manager of one of the banks in the town centre. 'Towers Towers' we called Dick's luxurious dwelling. We often ended up there after the pub or at my house which was a far less spacious alternative. In truth, I sometimes found these friends tedious company. But if there wasn't a dance on anywhere, it was Hobson's choice. Either go out with them to the Brunswick, where we could get served, or stay in and watch the television with my family. Simon could sometimes instigate a bit of political debate by regurgitating views expressed in his father's Daily Telegraph. And Dick had a slightly more adventurous streak in him than the others, even if it was wrapped up in a lot of fussy and conformist procedures that he had picked up at Sea Scouts. None of them had a girlfriend nor ever had yet as far as I knew. At least, I kept making an effort in that respect.

In the school assembly our headmaster Geoffrey McPherson MA (Oxon) - Geo McPherson for short or, to be even more abbreviated, Gopher - expanded upon his grand plan for the fifty mile walk. Preparation was essential and Mr Michaelson, who was also a captain in the school's army cadet force, was commandeered to give specialist advice. Stout walking boots were essential. Plimsolls totally inappropriate. Things called blisters were probably the greatest enemy, contesting that position only with something known as low moral fibre. Acting on these recommendations, I bought a bottle of white spirit from the hardware shop and, for a few evenings before the walk, rubbed this into my feet after washing them in a bowl of hot water.

On the big day, I joined the crowd on the seafront at a quarter to six with the dawn still to creep in across the bay, having walked from home thus notching up a first, extra mile already. I sought out Dick who was with his parents at the road side with their car while others stood about in groups with vacuum flasks or khaki knapsacks. The air was full of hearty laughter and raised voices insensitive to the stillness of early morning on the levelled water. Mr Michaelson's bonhomie and encouragement seemed forced and paternalistic and I was relieved when Gopher stepped up to cut a white ribbon that had been stretched out between two prefects.

'The best of luck to you all,' he said. 'Let's show everybody what the school can do.'

For the first few miles, the string of walkers along the main road was concentrated enough for Dick and myself to be able to hear the banter from in front and behind. Over this first hour, the dawn gained a presence, rendering the orange light from the sodium lamps superfluous. I concentrated on keeping my stride regular and purposeful and was surprised soon to find myself as far from home as I had ever wandered on foot. The line of walkers began to extend in length as it crawled upwards towards the hairpin bend on the road that crested the Ridgeway hills.

After eight miles we skirted Dorchester, Hardy's Casterbridge, as the streets were becoming busier with people engaged in regular morning routines, the commonplace separated from us by some transparent but impenetrable screen. Dick and I agreed to walk at our own pace, perhaps to reunite further on in the day, and he then began to draw ahead of me as our route turned eastwards towards the fully risen sun.

Just a mile or so outside the town, I crossed an old stone bridge, the water in the small stream beneath almost hidden beneath a tangle of crowfoot and water cress. Here, or certainly hereabouts, Fanny Robin had collapsed exhausted as she dragged herself, heavily pregnant, towards the garrison town in search of Sergeant Troy. The fictional resonated deeply for me, the jingoistic pride driving this walk and my exhibitionist vanity seemed far less worthy and more contrived.

Such musings increased as I moved further into territory that was new to me and I was only shocked from my silent soliloquies by the sudden shriek of a car horn close behind me. It was Ernie and the others in his parents' car.

'Up the workers!' shouted one of them.

'Onward Christian soldiers!' another.

I was cheered by the moment of companionship but irritated by their clichéd immaturity. Within a very short time, however, I then began to feel deflated by the thought that I too could be cruising along on an upholstered car seat.

All morning in the long lead up to lunchtime, following a bearing that carried me further and further from our starting point and all familiar landmarks, I was sustained by reverie and thoughts of eventually turning towards home at Lytchett Matravers. Here I would stop for lunch and here, when I did finally arrive, I found Dick with three prefects and Mr Michaelson dispensing bluff, good cheer and cups of coffee.

We had been advised during preparation for the walk not to sit down at rest breaks so I forced myself to remain standing while I ate the cheese and pickle sandwiches that my mother had packed into an old knapsack borrowed from Dick. The two of us then set off, agreeing to stay together to bolster each other's determination, knowing that the miles, past the thirty and then the forty mark and then still more, would gorge themselves on our very last drops of strength and resolve.

We passed Wareham after another hour or so as I occupied myself with calculations, proportions of the journey completed and remaining and the likely times of arrival at various landmarks. Out of time with my forced footfalls, the numbers floated in an unfocused mist, dissolving each time I neared an answer.

On a minor road somewhere close by, TE Lawrence had lost control of his motor cycle, had parted man from machine as each grazed and sparked furiously across the asphalt on their separate, final trajectories. Today the road beneath my boots seemed solid and malevolent as if pushing up deliberately to compact the bones of my shins and thighs.

Up ahead, swaying from side to side and shuffling onwards alone, was a boy called Robert whom everybody knew as Crinkle because of his wiry, frizzled hair. He was an isolated and not particularly popular member of the sixth form. His father was a local dignitary, the managing director of a large nautical engineering firm that was the region's largest employer. It was commonly believed that some favouritism or special link had been behind Crinkle being allowed to stay on at school to sit his A-levels for an unprecedented third time in an attempt to raise his grades.

Out here on the road though, yoked together in weariness, we were all three equally exhausted and walked onwards in silent determination. At the top of a slight rise in the road we could see a perfectly positioned bench facing south west. From here, under the fading afternoon sun, the town was distantly visible, Portland a brooding hulk, huge and sullen in the sea beyond. We debated the wisdom of sitting down and decided that nothing, not fatigue, cramp nor blistered feet, could now prevent us from completing the remaining miles.

As we sat, saying little but savouring each numb second of our ten minute rest, a grey Wolseley pulled up the incline towards us and indicated its intention of stopping.

'Oh God! It's Gopher,' said Dick.

The last time, the only time in fact, that I had spoken individually with Gopher was nine months earlier, a humbling request made in his office at the end of the summer holidays. I had promised to apply myself more fully and improve upon my pitiable 'O-level' results if I could be allowed to stay on at school and enter the sixth form. Gopher had listened without expression, his eyes magnified by his spectacle lenses, the dimple in the centre of his chin pulling in my attention like a whirlpool. I was asked to repeat my surname as he hitched the dusty black gown back up across his shoulders and then ran his finger down the left hand column on a large sheet of paper on the desk in front of him. Stopping about half way, he placed a foot ruler on the page and followed it across a number of columns with his index finger. He cleared his throat and said that my performance marked me out as somebody the school would not normally consider to be 'sixth form material'. And then as I hung my head he stipulated the degree of application and sheer hard work that would be the condition for granting my request. When asked if I understood, I forced a 'Yes, sir' trying hard to make this assent sound more than a resentful grunt.

Now, Gopher was walking towards us slapping his rolled up driving gloves into the palm of his left hand. He was wearing a pullover with a cravat beneath an open shirt, the first time I had ever seen him without a collar and tie. His gaze settled on Crinkle whom he approached first.

'How are you, Robert?' asked Gopher, smiling encouragingly. 'Only another seven miles. Keep at it, you're nearly there'.

'Yes sir,' replied Crinkle meekly, gazing at his feet as if in shame.

'And Towers,' he said, working his way along the line. 'Good lad, keep it up. Back to it!'

'Yes sir,' said Dick, still able to summon an enthusiastic and open grin.

'And, eh, how about you ... um?' he asked, turning towards me. 'No sitting about. Not the time to give up now.'

But it was. Dick and Crinkle pulled themselves back onto their feet, groaning from their aches and placing their weight carefully onto the sensitive soles of their feet. Not one spark, however, fired through my being. The other two made feeble proclamations of worthy intentions while the late afternoon air pressed heavily onto my eyes and ears and I lost the struggle to remember who I was and where I had mislaid my very last scrap of self-belief.

Telling You How To Live

Something like The Beatles or The Rolling Stones. Not an obvious copy but something that would look exciting and attention-grabbing on posters or noticeboards outside a dance hall. In the charts even.

Our group needed a name.

Paul suggested The Foursome but the rest of us found that too limp. Derek came up with The Groovers which we thought was better but still not exactly what we wanted.

We had been practicing in our front room and at Derek's house for nearly three months and were proud of the repertoire we had built up, three songs from *'Please Please Me'*, two from the charts and a few rhythm and blues numbers that Paul had learned from his uncle's collection. Spider's dad had bought him a new drum set and carried it to practices in his works van, scowling at the rest of us whenever he unloaded the kit into our houses.

When the amplifier was switched on echoing feedback would wobble across the room, threatening to break some kind of sound barrier. I loved the deep rounded hum from warming valves and the matter-of-fact, technical smell of electrical dust. The shrieking sound from one plucked guitar string could be too loud for our ears, intense enough it seemed to prise the plaster from the walls.

We made plans, it was a period of great ambition. We talked about the route to bookings for local dances and Spider suggested his dad as a possible manager because of the business knowledge he had acquired from running his grocery shop. We talked about semi-professional status and whether we might have to leave school when we reached that stage. We talked a lot. And all the while nobody directly confronted the fact that I couldn't play a musical instrument.

Something that should have been natural was missing. Instead of providing an easy rhythm, my guitar strumming created crashing sounds out of time, ruining the songs. Spider had already claimed the drums so I ended up with a special harmonica that played chords. All that should have been required from me was a chugging accompaniment formed from alternating breaths in and out. But even with this simplest of instruments my weedy, wheezing contribution remained an embarrassment.

I was sure that the others must have been wondering how to tell me that I was no asset to them. They might well have had their eyes on other potential and more promising replacements. And when the group landed a first booking to play at the lower sixth Easter party, I knew that a reckoning was being forced.

So I took preemptive action, announcing my decision first to my parents, to their obvious delight

'I've decided to give up the group so that I can concentrate more on my A-levels'.

To Paul, Derek and Spider I presented a different rationale

'I just think folk is the way it is going. That's more the scene I want to get into'.

And there was some truth to both claims. Records by the Kingston Trio and Peter, Paul and Mary, among others, were being played more often on the radio and I found their melody-driven narratives particularly attractive. I had even located a monthly folk club that was advertised in a pub up by the railway station and persuaded Paul to come with me one Saturday night.

He was not too impressed by the atmosphere he said. The long narrow back bar was laid out with small round tables and at many of these three or four people were sat on stools. At the far end was an unraised stage area and when we entered with our glasses of lemonade the room was in complete silence except for the singing of a man with a dark beard and chunky green cardigan. He played no instrument but his strong clear voice, as if powered by his bulky frame, filled the room with the story of a woman's lover who had been tricked into enlisting in some historical war.

I recognised this as the type of song Bob Dylan talked about when people yelled 'Judas' at him for abandoning the musical persona of a folky, solitary, guitar-strumming troubadour. They were enraged by his transformation into a stick thin figure screaming with electricity about the distortion of feeling and authenticity in a society knotted up and twisted out of shape by paranoia, fear and greed. In reply, he defended his roots

'All these songs about roses growing out of people's brains and lovers who are really geese and swans that turn into angels – they're not going to die'.

That evening in the folk club, we heard many such songs, some of which invited our mumbled contributions to their choruses. Many of the people in the audience were older than us but certainly younger than our parents. Unlike the darkened dance halls where we usually spent our evenings when the opportunity arose, this room was fully lit.

Paul did not want to return the following month but I had felt comfortable enough to go there by myself the next time. I was impressed by the singers' easy relationships with their audience, in fact by the lack of a firm demarcation between performer and listener. As the evening progressed one became the other, as various people stood to take their turn. Two girls not much older than me made a striking impression. A darker haired, shorter one picked out a guitar accompaniment where every note shone true. Her taller friend had the longest hair I had ever seen, ash blonde and completely straight almost to her waist. She stood erect with a startling confidence and sang to the back wall of the room.

They buried her in the old church yard
Sweet William lay beside her
And from his heart grew a red, red rose
And out of hers, a briar.

Songs about fishing for the whale, shipwrecks and sailors returning in disguise after years at sea to test a lover's faithfulness. Escaping slaves following the drinking gourd. Enclosure of the land, press gangs and country boys lured into joining up. The callous indifference of generals, disasters at the mine, the dust bowls, strikes and scabs. Rebels hung on the Bridge of Toome.

The Bomb, the fallout shelter, love grasped in the moment. The assassinations, marches and solidarity. Life and loyalty at the margins, voices raised together, the peace-mongers

His 'catechism' Dylan called them. *'Songs that could tell you how to live'.*

The turning of the seasons, gentlemen of the open road, blossoms and garlands, the lark and the dove. High days and festivals, May Day, jigs and reels, the harvest, the winter feast, the wassail.

Some of these were songs with echoes of those I had heard and hated years before at primary school. Songs that had retained their husk and grain though, had not been ground and smoothed into a paste for easy consumption. Undimmed and undiminished despite the decades and the centuries.

They grew and grew in the old church yard
'Til they could grow no higher
And at the top twined in a lover's knot,
The rose around the briar.

Gainful Employment

'But George Orwell had something to fall back on. He had money behind him'.

I didn't want to admit it but I could see that my Dad might be right. Washing up day in day out might eventually get boring.

But what about W. H. Davies? '*The Autobiography of a Super Tramp*' had been so persuasive. The company of honest souls, straightforward people with simple needs. The dignity and honest fatigue from physical labour, the scholarly volume for secret study stashed inside a bedroll.

This was my own decision though, the first time I wasn't going along with somebody else telling me what I ought to be doing. How could being an apprentice draughtsman, my Dad's suggestion, bring any meaningful and deep fulfillment? Guaranteed employment, enforced conformity, marriage to a local girl who worked in a shop. Fifty years of that!

I told my father that I wanted to be a tramp, an intellectual one. I could so clearly imagine myself at reading tables in public libraries, working my way methodically along the stacks. I would be warm and dry. I wouldn't want for anything more. And I would learn infinitely more than I ever could from grinding on through a final year with 'A' levels.

'And where would you sleep?'

'In hedges and fields. Wherever I ended up that night'.

'Don't talk so wet'.

But it must be possible. Davies and Orwell had managed through the storms, the rain and the snow. Had written the books to prove it. All it needed was some of the initiative that school and my Dad were always on about - the officer material stuff, the leadership potential. But not in the service of Queen and country, respectability and a soulless life. In the pursuit of poetry instead, philosophy, the camaraderie of the trail, the grit, grime and freedom of voyages without destinations.

*

South Dorset Gazette   *22nd June 1964*

'Mohairs' get a welcome cuppa

Weymouth has always been famous for its record numbers of summer visitors. But this year a new group of arrivals has set local people talking.

The 'Mohairs' – so called because they have 'more hair' than the average person – are a group of young people who arrived in the town in May after being cleared out from St Ives, Cornwall, following a purge by the local town council. There are some 15 to 20 of them currently here but the town has been warned that many more could be expected if the word gets around that Weymouth offers them a warm welcome.

Pictured enjoying a cup of tea at the Early Bird Café on Park Street is Mohair Sammy Easterman, 20, originally from Birmingham. He is currently looking for temporary holiday work and says he will consider anything, from lavatory cleaner to bank manager. He adds 'It's a free country and we just want to live our lives in the way that we want to'

Also pictured is Albert Watts, proprietor of the Early Bird cafe.

'A lot of people don't like the look of the

Mohairs, but they should take the trouble to get to know them. Under the surface, there are some very nice young people here and they will always be welcome in my café,' Mr Watts told the Gazette.

'Older people only think about material possessions and mortgages and things,' said Linda, another Mohair from the West Midlands, who did not want to give her age or surname.

'Weymouth is rightly proud of its reputation as the ideal holiday resort for families and people of all ages,' said Cllr Frederick Watson, Chair of the Tourism and Leisure Sub-committee of Weymouth Town Council. 'We have been placed in the top ten British seaside towns for the past five years running. The Council will be monitoring the situation with these young people very carefully,' he told the Gazette.

---

*

In late July that summer, I obtained a job in the kitchen of the Solent Hotel up on the seafront. On my first day, I was shown around, my basic duties were explained and I was set to work to pull up the dishes from the floor below by means of the dumb waiter. In the open lift shaft, the top of the wooden case creaked upwards only minimally despite all my pulling and I wondered whether I had the strength for the job.

'Here, let's give you a hand,' said one of the kitchen staff and, with him also pulling firmly on the rope, we managed to raise the contraption further. Our final attempts lifted the open fronted box up to the level of the hatch. But, instead of plates, compacted inside and inches in front of me, knees up to his chin like a foetus and with a long kitchen knife between his teeth, was a wild-haired, mad-eyed homunculus. It was Sammy, the Mohair whose photograph I had seen in the newspaper. When others had eased him out, he ran about the kitchen, bent at the knees, the knife now waving in the air.

The others stood back to allow his manic passage as he slashed at the air mimicking a crazed pirate. After a circuit of the central aluminium storage unit with the others laughing but allowing him a considerable berth, he stopped right in front of me. Still crouching low, he turned one eye upwards. It seemed bulbous beneath his spectacles and somehow swollen larger than the other.

'What brings you here? Are you friend or foe? Answer for your life!'

I struggled to match the mood and find the words, unsure whether I should speak at all. Then the swing doors to the corridor burst inwards and a tall moon-faced man entered, stiff legged and swaying slightly from side to side. He was dressed in a gold lame suit and wore a large stetson hat. His hands were making circular movements as if twirling six guns.

'Just back off from the boy and put down the knife,' he drawled.

The laughter intensified, splitting into an echoing gaggle of shrieks and yells.

'Come on, I'll show you what to do,' said a quieter man in a brown T-shirt and denim jeans. 'I'm the other washer-upper, Billy. Don't worry, they do that to all the new people, it's nothing personal'.

'We have a laugh here,' he added. 'Most of them are alright. Just one or two you need to look out for'.

I was introduced to the first laugh early the next morning in the rush to prepare breakfast for some eighty guests. Sammy, still an unpredictable character, shouted from the bank of gas rings near the serving surfaces, a raised sticky ladle in his right hand.

'Porridge is ready!'

'Come on, get in the queue,' said Billy as people lined up beside the large cauldron of molten porridge that burped and belched occasionally in the pan.

'Okay,' said Sammy. One of the waiters was first in line and he came forward, bent over the pot and pretended to spit into it. One by one, kitchen porters and waiters stepped up beside Sammy, acknowledged his lop-sided grin and made their donation to the pot. I was trapped and had to comply as they all watched me, the new boy. I gave a limp imitation, nothing compared to the exaggerated hawking and retching of some who provoked squeals of appreciation and mock disgust, but I seemed to pass the test.

'I can't see what's so good about a crowd of layabouts,' my Dad said when I enthused at home about my new workmates.

'But they're real people, Dad,' I complained. 'Billy's even been in prison but he's really kind. And genuine'.

'Genuine? You want to watch yourself or you'll end up in the clink with them'.

One morning, after I had been at the Solent for a week, one of the younger waiters approached me in the corridor.

'Are you the grammar school boy who's working here?' He spoke in the broadest Irish accent I had ever heard. 'What do you study?'

I told him it was maths and physics but did not mention my disappointing GCE results and the fact that I had only just scraped into the sixth form.

'No philosophy, no literature?' he fired back. 'Do you study Plato? Euripides? And what about Irish writers?

Shaw, Wilde and Yeats?'

'Our school doesn't do philosophy,' I replied 'but I have done a bit for myself'.

'What? What did you read?'

'I got Gilbert Ryle's *'A Concept of Mind'* out of the library last year'.

'What did you think of it? What struck you the most about it?'

'Well, I didn't read all of it, mainly the first few chapters. I remember it was something about what's real and things. About perception and stuff'.

'Huh. Metaphysical ramblings. You need Joad, *'An Introduction to Philosophy'*. It's a *'Teach Yourself'* book. It'll get you started. And literature. Shaw's *'Man and Superman'* probably. And what about Thoreau? *'Walden'*. You must read that straight away, before anything else. Oh, and Colin Wilson, *'The Outsider'*.

My new personal tutor – there had been no opportunity to decline the rapidly lengthening reading list – was called Bernard. He was only a couple of years older than me and dressed conservatively in dark trousers and a long-sleeved white shirt. He had dark hair, already slightly graying and combed sideways with a cartoon-like set of rippling small waves. He and his friend Nick had come to Weymouth following the clear out from St Ives earlier that summer. Their plan was to move on at the end of the summer season to spend the winter in London and then the following spring in Montmartre where Bernard intended to settle as a full-time painter.

After my first pay day, Bernard came with me to W H Smiths where we presented a list of books to an attractive girl with long blonde hair who had been in the year below me at school.

'We don't have any of these in stock but we can order them for you,' she said, giving no indication that she recognised me as she consulted a large, well-thumbed catalogue.

Bernard advised which should be asterisked as priorities. The assistant remained immune to the list's aura of gravity.

When the books finally arrived I decided to tackle Thoreau first, drawn by the title and even more by the tone of rebellion in the title of the final extended essay, '*On Civil Disobedience*'. The text was dense and there was no respite in levity or short, snappy sentences. But I was determined that this was to be a period of study unlike all those before when my attention had rushed in every direction except along the lines of a text book's printed sentences. This would not culminate in another humiliation stretched across slow, silent hours in an examination hall.

'I've never read anything like this before,' I said one day at home of Joad's 'Introduction to Philosophy'. It makes you question everything, everything you've just taken for granted'.

'Don't read it then if it's upsetting you,' said my Mum. 'Read something else instead'.

'It's not upsetting me. It's the most amazing – '

'It's a pity you can't show the same enthusiasm about something that might actually help you get a job when you leave school,' interjected my Dad.

I held back a furious desire to scream that the human race could never hope to improve itself in the face of such … such … I didn't know what.

Over the next few weeks, Bernard and I occupied ourselves with our books in between shifts, first in the Early Bird Café and then, when the proprietor announced that he was banning 'low-life' from his premises, tucked away at the back of Fortes Corner House in the centre of the town. Bernard would open his creased and battered copy of the volume under consideration to reveal sections of ink and pencil underlining. Never before had bookish analysis possessed such dramatic import for me, - the writer as revolutionary, the reader as acolyte. I lost myself among outsiders, wanderers and seekers and left my former school friends to their bars and dance halls. My ignorance and lack of application were revealed by questions that I now longed to be able to answer.

'What are the deep themes?' 'How does the author bring home his argument?'

I also took to underlining as I read and my pages were soon extensively scored with only occasional passages left white and unmarked like glimpses of accidentally revealed flesh.

Returning home one night after a dizzying extended tutorial spent scrutinising the preface to Shaw's 'Man and Superman,' I found Uncle Sid sitting with my parents in the living room.

Both my parents spoke of Sid with an unqualified affection. He worked as a gardener and wore checked open-necked shirts, a slowly weathered tan and a wide smile. When a meal was placed before him he looked down at it in silent pleasure as if saying a personal grace before starting to eat. When beckoned to an armchair in front of the television, he approached it with what seemed a glowing and genuine gratitude.

Somehow that evening I found myself quickly on from stilted pleasantries.

'But if I'm looking at something, this tomato for instance, and I'm seeing what I think of as the redness of it, what I'm really seeing is rays of light coming off this thing and striking my eyes which then get transmitted to my brain and that sensation in my brain is what I call the redness'.

Sid seemed to be following, his head was bent forward slightly.

'Now, what we don't know, is whether exactly the same is happening in your brain. You're getting your own rays striking your eyes which are then going through to your brain and creating what you call redness. But what we don't know, is whether your redness is the same as mine. How can we? We just assume they're the same and we use the same words but that doesn't mean that anybody's experience of redness is the same as anybody else's. We have absolutely no way of knowing'.

'Well, I don't know, Andrew,' said Sid. 'You make it all sound so complicated. All I know is that that tomato is red, that's it really'.

'But that's my point. You don't know that! Well, you don't know that it's the same as what I call 'red''.

Sid looked even sadder and my father quickly intervened, silencing the evening.

'He's going through one of those phases,' he said sharply. 'Reading Bertrand Russell and what have you. They all go through it'.

Above and Beyond

At 16, I joined St Mary's church youth club down among the tightly terraced houses near the railway station, not to find God but to meet girls.

I had given up on religion a few years earlier after regular stints of Sunday school and church at St Oswalds, nearer my home. When I had complained about this enforced attendance, which I felt marked my brother and I out from all the other children on the Shorehaven estate, my mother always said I could decide for myself when I was thirteen. Apparently this was my father's stipulation although I had never actually known him to enter a church. On the stroke of my designated spiritual maturation I consequently made a rapid departure.

My mother arranged flowers in St Oswalds and washed the altar steps. Glimpses of the curate, Father Schofield, floating through the vestry replenished her emotionally whilst also agitating her compassion beyond its easy or comfortable expression. He was a tiny, fleshless man, sometimes seeming little more than a loose collection of bones somehow held together beneath his cassock. He had been a Japanese prisoner of war my mother informed me. And as I watched him move silently among his rituals, I tried to imagine the squalor and the blows that might have been inflicted on him in the wet heat of a jungle camp.

Father Schofield's humility and dignity suggested that he had found a balm for his wounds and I knew that he would remain in my thoughts. But otherwise I felt only relief at getting away from the stifling respectability exuded by his superior, the vicar, a well-fed career clergyman who preached cloying and clichéd sermons and presided over sickly summer fetes.

My friend, Dick, told me that the girls at St Mary's youth club were less restrained than our grammar school contemporaries but that the price to be paid for access to these temptations was the mid-evening coffee break. At around half past eight, Bob, the young curate who ran the club, began scraping the wooden chairs back into rows, barring the clanking, heavy exit door with no more than a keen eye and a chilling charm. The tap and cluck from the table tennis room died away and we sat, avoiding his glance, beneath the buzz of a yellow strip light while Bob dispensed spiritual guidance for the regulation fifteen minutes.

Wearingly-familiar Bible stories gained some lift, however, when Bob forced them into the world we tried to claim as ours. Frank had been coming to know the Lord, he told us, he really had, in the days before his huge Norton roared from the road splintering a row of fence posts before its fatal impact with the telegraph pole. And the evening the snooker tables crashed onto their sides and the billiard balls ricocheted and whined against the tiled walls and flagstone floors, Bob strode between them parting the sea of missiles. He halted hostilities by dragging out a large, dusty gymnasium mat, as brown and bristly as a fox. 'Queensberry rules chaps. No punching or biting, no knees and no hitting below the belt'. First he took on one ringleader, circling in an almost polite fashion until the first engagement, the assault on balance, the thud of bodies against the floor, the assertion of strength and the weakening in one shoulder and then the other. Afterwards, blood, sweat, spittle and torn clothes with Bob extending a handshake, wiping his mouth and then turning to repeat his challenge to the other gang leader.

No milk and water respectability this. No Holy Joe, genteel and practised among his catechisms.

Bob could not have been more different from the clergy I had known at St Oswalds. His curriculum vitae was transcribed directly from the adventure stories of my childhood – public school, Cambridge, the Marines with whom he had crossed the Sahara and become a rock climber and mountaineer. Divinity college. Not one glimpse of any such experiences in all my years growing up in Purbeck Road, nor across the whole of the Shorehaven Estate. My friend Dick and I became willing recruits as seconds on the rope as Bob explored the untouched sea cliffs at Lulworth Cove and Portland. We were conscientious students in matters of the waist belay and bowline, the three points of contact with the rock, the careful footwork and the superiority of balance over brute strength.

He sparred, to my delight, in the correspondence columns of the South Dorset Gazette with Mr Price, the local coast guard:

sheer irresponsibility, treacherous terrain, endangering others
versus
the spiritual need for unimpeded adventure, the full exploration of one's limits.

The thrill of debate, the ripostes and the counter-arguments.

over-stretched rescue services, the duty to set an example
clashing directly with
teamwork, skills chiseled during disciplined apprenticeships, the testing of character.

I had always avoided clubs and organisations designed to deliver a disciplined experience of adventure to young people. The enthusiasts for the Scouts I had known in my younger years seemed most often to be the boys with a profligate strength, the fighters. The later enthusiasts for the Duke of Edinburgh award, on the other hand, were the supporters of order and leadership, of Queen, country and the responsibly-constructed outdoor latrine.

Perhaps it was the daily expounding of my father's too ready support for his wartime experiences in the RAF, the imposition of a firm military order giving him the best days of his life. Or maybe it was my mother's unhappy experiences with the various church clubs and societies she enthusiastically signed up for only to scurry quickly away after some early tiff or altercation with another of their members. But whatever made me wary and suspicious did not apply out on the cliffs.

Standing with Dick on a small ledge above a sullen, restless sea on one of our first trips, no escape but upwards, I could hear Bob above us hammering in a piton that would provide a secure anchor for the three of us, his voice booming in full song and the blows of metal on metal providing cold chinks of accompaniment.

'For - those - in – thwack – per – il – thwack – on – the sea - thwack'.

Here was adventure devoid of the smothering oversight of institutions. No packs, or troops or gangs. High stakes on walls of sea-scoured limestone. No hierarchies, no accrediting bodies, the only disciplinary forces, God and gravity.

Only in his mid-twenties, hospital visiting and a subsidiary role at evening service were insufficient to keep Bob in Weymouth and he was away within a year or so to the new challenge of running a Boys Club in Bermondsey. A year later, aged seventeen, Dick and I hitched there. Along the line of shuttered warehouses down from Tower Bridge at night, Earth had not anything to show more menacing or more frightening. In an empty light early the next morning, the city already in motion along its streets and river, we each requisitioned a best fit set of equipment from the club's store room – boots, anorak, sleeping bag and inflatable mattress – and set the compass further north, the furthest in this direction ever for me, to the recently opened M1. On this superhighway we took account of the complex new regulations my father had warned me about. 'Apparently, once you're on it, that's it. You can't change your mind and turn round'.

Running in his new yellow Ford Anglia at speeds never in excess of forty miles an hour, we were heading into thinly sketched mountain marvels. The fourth member of our party was Eric, a young man probably no more than ten years our senior, whom Bob had first met as a regular inmate on his rounds of visiting at Dorchester gaol.

After a whole day, we arrived in Snowdonia. Driving through the Nant Ffrancon Pass, looking for the track down to our barn, massive hillsides rose in slides of scree and rubble above the single road. Buttresses of the deepest Celtic green, rough ground tumbling out of the mist and down to the valley floor, these were landscapes beyond anything I had ever imagined. Our base - our lives - for the next week.

Eric's eyes followed another waterfall upwards, its source hidden in the sky.

'Thuck-in nell, Bob. Look at those bath-tuds'.

Silence from the driver. Mortification from the other passengers.

'Caw, thuck me!'

'Eric!'

'Nnn?'

'The ears, Eric. Getting a little red'.

'What? Oh! Oh, thuckin nell, Bob, thorry'.

All week heavy mist, cloud and rain dominated the valley. Each morning this weather made its insolent parade around and between the isolated farm dwellings and the bluffs of inhospitable ground. In the barn, we attempted to prepare meals over primus stoves, the smell of the meths never completely absent, the pans never fully free from the burned-on remnants of our previous efforts. Bob modelled orderly living among the privations. Each evening, after soakings and exhaustion on the hills, he led a session of prayers accompanied by mugs of cocoa. Nobody dared raise the possibility of a lift to the village pub.

On our final day, we attempted a rock climbing route on Lliwedd, a mountain composed of north-facing cliffs and buttresses. Some years later, when I met a wider circle of contemporary climbers, I learned that this abandoned place had once been a favoured haunt of that generation of pioneers from the 1920s and 1930s, men with a vanished ethic of risk and hardship.

We were only two or three rope lengths up the route, about two hundred and fifty feet, and I was standing alone in snow left over from the winter on a tiny ledge, when the exposure took a grip on me. To either side, un-climbable walls thinning out into nothingness. The line by which we had just ascended disappeared quickly into cloud beneath our feet. Improbably steep rocks above looked just passable, at least for the few feet into which visibility extended. As soon as somebody climbed into the mist, their voice was snatched away by the sideways buffeting of the wind. Out of contact, except for the wet rope around my back and wrists, the void in front and beneath, the hopeless features of the rock walls all around, I was incarcerated on this tiny, snowbound stance, held in by emptiness and despair.

As my turn to climb again arrived, my resolution dissolved into the vast indifference of the landscape, the dripping rock pillars, the patches of stale snow, the grey tumult above, below and to my sides. There was the best part of another thousand feet of this, continuing upwards, further and further from safe, solid ground. I was already shaking before the needles of cold again began to probe each point of entry into my clothing, shivering at the lost hope of ever feeling safe again. Part of me wanted to jump, to untie my waist belay and cast free, to end the accumulating sense of hopelessness. Part wanted to blame Bob or kick at the rock and withered heather. I could only just bite back the adolescent howl that said I wanted to end it all, a howl that nobody would hear.

When I reached Bob he was hunched up against the weather, bringing in the rope, and still smiling.

'I'm sorry, Bob. I can't .... I just don't think I can ...'

'Don't worry, Andy,' he shouted against the buffeting wind, although he was only a couple of feet from me on our tiny belay ledge.

'You can do it. God loves you'.

Concrete Proposal

'Creativity in Concrete'

That's what it said across the top. And then below, the soaring line of a bridge. Sculptured and white, stretching as far as a rainbow's end across a sky of brilliantly saturated blue. Nothing else, just this clean, perfect geometry.

At the bottom, the words 'Careers in Civil Engineering'.

We were in the sixth form hut. Mr Michaelson was distributing the green UCCA forms and the mood was subdued. Something serious was about to happen, something that was possibly irrevocable. And I had left it too late to find out what and to undertake preparatory action.

Although my friends and other kids in the sixth form talked about applying for university, my thoughts always wandered somewhere else at those times. In fact, my thoughts were not thoughts at all but a diffuse and comforting muzziness into which the sights and sounds of the outside world melted and became muted.

Friends said things like 'Sussex is supposed to be good for history' and it puzzled me. I knew roughly where Sussex was but not the nature of this purported link. Why not say, for example, with equal conviction that Dorset was good for history? For my parents and myself, grammar schools had been some way beyond our understanding, institutions that engendered our respect and also a little fear. Sixth forms were definitely foreign territory and anything further brought no image to mind.

My father tried to keep abreast of these matters and passed on what he had discovered to me.

'They do these three year sandwich courses where you do the theory at the university and have the middle one out in industry where you put it into practice'.

Industry! The word itself filled me with dread never mind having to turn up each morning at a factory. Chimneys belching out smoke, a decaying urban sprawl all around, clocking on, artificial light, the rumble of heavy machinery. I could happily sing along to 'Dirty Old Town' and feel the frisson of meeting my love by the gas works wall. I could even see that train set the night on fire. But actually believe that in less than a year I would be smelling the spring on the sulphur air? It was impossible.

Mr Michaelson was reminding us to read the instructions at the top of the green form carefully because it would not be possible to correct any errors later. There were boxes where we were required to enter the degree topic or topics of our choosing.

'What are you putting?' I asked Tony Bridges next to me. He had shown no hesitation when faced with the empty boxes.

'Civil engineering' he said in a worldly way.

'What's that?' I asked.

Without looking up from his paper, he reached into the breast pocket of his blazer and produced a folded leaflet, the one with the beautiful arc of a newly constructed suspension bridge spanning a pristine sky.

Creativity in concrete. It had a ring to it and my only other plans lacked any specificity. I had diffuse but intensely felt desires to spend my life among intellectuals, writers and artists. But, despite experiencing occasional shivers of excitement at one or two of Keats' metaphors or feeling terrified out on the marshes with Pip, I had failed miserably in my English

Literature 'O' level. I also longed to possess an overview of the huge historical forces that had shaped my world but had trouble distinguishing a Tudor from a Stuart, a Whig from a Tory. I was easily fired by political rhetoric and the plight of the underdog but had no appetite for local party meetings or parochial policy discussions. Again, I could imagine myself immersed for life in musical composition and performance but was unable to rub two notes together in tune.

Science subjects, physics and maths, were the only areas in which I could achieve some examination success. Or, to put it more honestly, these were the only fields in which I did not fail to reach a pass mark. Early in my sixth form career I had experienced the thrill of realising that universal laws were just that. They were universal. They could describe both the motion of the planets and the bucket of water that I swung around my head on the beach as a child. The invisible clockwork governing the universe. A moon could smash into its neighbouring planet in the same way that the water could fall from the pail onto my head. And - and this was the wonder of it - with some arithmetical calculations on a piece of paper we could calculate the tipping points for both. Even I could do that! I could defy the water and determine the course of the stars.

Creativity in concrete. The end of my search. The fusion I had been seeking suddenly, and in the nick of time, revealed.

Into the empty box on the sheet in front of me I inserted, in the specified black ink, the letters that I believed might seal my destiny:

C-I-V-I-L-E-N-G-I-N-E-E-R-I-N-G

*

With these forms completed and out of my hands, I felt freed from further nagging questions about my future. I had been required to nominate six establishments and had hedged my bets by choosing three of what I understood to be old and established universities and three of the newly-created colleges of advanced technology. Now I could leave this paperwork to complete its journey through a network of in-trays and filing cabinets in alien towns and cities across the country. Through the winter my commitment to my studies at school increased and I managed to find more focus, a concentration disrupted regularly though by music and thoughts of girls. But the numbing denial of what I was to do after leaving school could not last and early in the new year, I began to receive rejection letters from the higher education establishments that I had selected.

I might still believe that Gopher was mistaken when he had expressed doubts about my suitability for his sixth form. But these official letters dropping one by one on to our doormat certainly confirmed my fear that I was now attempting to reach beyond my abilities, beyond the modest ambitions of my family and beyond the painstakingly-mapped and familiar terrain of the Shorehaven Estate and our seaside paradise.

And then an acceptance. In the sixth buff envelope, an offer of a place, contingent only on the most basic of A-level passes. I had been accepted to study civil engineering at Salford College of Advanced Technology. I could retreat from unsteadying thoughts of the future back to the security of the present.

Apart from my climbing trip to Snowdonia a year or so earlier, the furthest north I had ever travelled was to Bristol once and London a couple of times. A quick check in an atlas revealed the complicated and extended hitch hiking route that would be needed to make a return visit home from Salford, a journey that might well not be possible in one day. So, I engaged myself even more fully with my A levels to the exclusion of these wider matters. But the deadline for my decision moved towards me under its own volition until I could avoid it no longer. I waited until the last possible day then, ignoring my father's warnings about birds in hands and bushes, I declined the place.

For the rest of the school year, while my friends made plans, I focused on a succession of more immediate landmarks – a dance on Friday, Easter holidays, asking a girl in the year below me to the pictures, my first A level exam and then each subsequent one. Acquiring a summer job, meeting my weekly deckchair sales. In this way, I managed to concern myself with the moment and nothing much more right through until the pinnacle of the town's tourism activity - August Bank Holiday Monday.

Records broken, temperatures soaring, the beach and promenade a dense swarm of bodies like a scuffed anthill or a disturbed colony of wasps. With every deckchair stack sold out, our thousands upon thousands of visitors spread themselves beneath the sun in a torpor or made their way between stalls and shops with slowed down movements, spreading sand across roads and pavements. Scurrying, quick and nimble, around and in among these huge crowds, local people attempted to cater for their every gaudy appetite and within those few peak weeks harvest an income that could be eked out across the remainder of the year.

But then, the lay-offs, those who had drifted into the town at the beginning of the summer floating away again into the margins of big cities elsewhere, friends packing cases and booking journeys, the rounds of good-byes and the ruddy enthusiasm for reunions. By the second week in September, I was one of the few employees remaining and attempting to sell a few nine-penny deckchair tickets. On a particularly wet Sunday, my father came along the promenade with a copy of the Sunday Times under his raincoat.

'There's a list here of all the courses that still have vacancies for this year,' he said, awakening in me a queasy feeling that the bustle of the summer had managed to suppress.

'Don't go turning your nose up at it,' he added. 'You say you want to go to London, well there's places in London on this list.'

The deserted beach had been freshly raked and aerated by a council vehicle that morning and the light rain that was now falling dimpled the surface with soggy pin pricks. I was aware of the concern behind my father's actions but was too absorbed in my own confusion and apprehension to appreciate or even acknowledge his efforts. I took the paper and stored it in our works cloakroom before returning to my stretch of promenade chairs. The weather had driven away my only customers, a small group of elderly ladies on a day trip from Crewkerne, so I passed the time until my lunch break throwing a stick that a sodden black Labrador had brought up from the beach and dropped at my feet. The dog raced with enthusiasm and without tiring up and down the ramp onto the beach, impervious to the deadening mood created by the wet mist blowing in across the bay. I needed to make a decision and take some action. To commit to the next step.

The next day, aware that my final pay packet was only

a week away, I gathered together a shilling's worth of pennies and walked round to the telephone box outside the shop on Mendip Street. After rehearsing my opening question until I felt confident, I made the long distance call to London.

The conversation was brief and successful. I would be in London within the week, sleeping at night on a settee in the library of Bob's boys club in Bermondsey and walking the streets of south east London by day looking in newsagents' windows for lodgings in a more convenient location.

I would live far beyond the unchanging skyline of hills that held in my home town. I would leave behind the seas that massaged our shores daily with every tide. I was impatient with the familiar, hemmed in by security. I would come alive in the anonymity of the city, alert to its dangers and unpredictability.

I dared to hope that my place to study civil engineering at Woolwich Polytechnic would at last provide my entrée into the world of poets and philosophers.

1983 – 1987

As Long as Everyone's Alright

'Dad says I shouldn't have told you. I mustn't say anything else'.

It was December 27th, 1983. My mother and I were back in the kitchen again doing the dishes after tea while the others settled in the living room to the television or the new toys. The computer, the Sinclair Spectrum, was dormant now, disconnected and inert on the kitchen table. I had been wondering all day when I might get the next opportunity to speak with my mother. Down in Buxton's Pavilion Gardens, my two older sons had raced around the ornamental landscape, disappointed that there had been no snow over Christmas but shouting to their grandparents to watch them swing on trees, career down a slippery bank, test out their footing on the rocks across the culvert. I had held my youngest son's hand whilst my parents admired and shouted. 'Watch out!'

'Oh, my godfathers, he'll be in there, I can't bear to look'. 'That's him to a tee, always a little monkey'.

We might have very little time. The pull of the computer had been intense, there had been hardly a moment when the rubber keys were not being stabbed or when the slow connection to the cassette player was not flickering away, downloading.

'Dad says it was wrong to tell you. You mustn't say anything to your brother'.

It had been the same the evening before, an explosive flash flood with events and memories careering past as my mother and I stood in the kitchen washing up after Boxing Day tea. It was only supposed to have been a casual enquiry in an attempt to tidy a few footnotes in my curiosity before the real work, if there were subsequently to be any, could begin. There had been two recent television series about tracing family trees and both took a diligent and reverential approach. Like Songs of Praise, wholesome and reassuring. It was said to provide a fascinating insight into the unwritten history of ordinary life down the ages. For those with the will and aptitude, here was an invitation to the famous, huge archives in London. Or, age-weathered parish records could be accessed in out of the way village churches, with a system of charges constructed around half crowns and guineas, and turn-around times for correspondence stretching into many months.

Not for me really. I could see the appeal of securing my family and myself within the branches and twigs of the centuries, but this was a world of cardigans, old books and a slowed-down appreciation of the delicately savoured fact. I had a full-time job as an educational psychologist, a young family, a rock climbing hobby and friends, all deserving more of my attention already.

Not yet, except for the one injunction:

'If you are thinking of doing this, talk to your oldest surviving relative today. Don't wait until tomorrow, do it today!'

So I told my mother that I was thinking of tracing our ancestors. She often talked of her earlier life, creating vivid pictures of herself as, for instance, a giggling schoolgirl crammed with others into bathing machines on Weymouth beach, struggling out from school uniforms and into one piece swimming costumes, to balance and tiptoe, suppressing squeals, out along the slippery struts shelving into the sea. Or, the night in the war when the land mine exploded on the beach, the sky shaking with orange fire, a thunderous crater on the sands right in front of the gracious, Georgian facade of our seafront hotels. 'They were after the dockyards, see, and Portland Harbour'. As a child this history had pulled itself about in my contemplation - bathing machines from the very earliest black and white photographs in history books or from the novels of Thomas Hardy, somehow jostling with the murderously modern and metallic.

Then there were the people, her relatives. Old Salisbury Granny, my mother's granny. She was totally blind and had a terrible time with Grandad, her husband, I was often told. He led her a right dance at times apparently but he couldn't help it. 'Poor old Salisbury Granny'. She was lovely, my mother said, so calm and patient. Poor as church mice. My mother as a young girl had to place money carefully in her hand - 'Fetch me my purse, Dot, I want to see what I've got' - so that she could palm the coins.

Mum's grandad had been in the Boer War. 'That was the cause of it all' my mother said. 'He was a proper old soldier'. I heard many times of the day he told her Granny he was going out for cigarettes, only to board the bus for Weymouth, all of forty miles away, to end up on the Esplanade marching back and forth all on his own in front of the military band performing for the holiday makers. 'He led poor Granny a dance'. The bus route to Weymouth wandered over dusty whaleback ridges and through empty Dorset farm country. Hours and hours he was gone. It was an unimaginable distance to me at the time, him so far from Granny's orderly surrounds, so helplessly available for the crowds' amusement. 'As soon as he heard a band, he was up there, swinging his arms'. My mother would swing hers too, even march about before me sometimes, as she recreated him. 'I'm just going out for some cigarettes, Queenie - that's what he called her, Queenie - I won't be long'.

I imagined Mum's grandad nimble and alive within the music, in scarlet with gold buttons like a Chelsea Pensioner, defiantly on parade up before the Jubilee Clock. This tower with its four clock faces, a blue and red column with ornate gold brocade, could be seen from the entrance to the railway station. It heralded the approach to the grand and trivial escapes offered by the sand and sea. The pompous thump of the brass band, the children's release on the crowded beach, gulls and the breezy crests on tiny waves in the shallows, all bolstering the frothy business of being alive. Word somehow reached my mother's family that he was there, all the way from Salisbury, up on the Prom. Somebody had seen him marching back and forth in front of the Jubilee Clock, with everybody laughing, and him oblivious. 'And poor old Granny worried sick about where he was'.

I knew these stories well, these people. I imagined their faces in my childhood in a later century. I walked through the same landscapes. But these two, my Mum's grandparents, belonged to an era as distant as the historical wars of the Crimea and Transvaal. The television programmes had helped me realise that there were others closer in time to me, others I should have known far better who were missing and unmentioned.

'I never knew Dad's mum, did I? I've always assumed she died before I was born?'

'Dad's mother died a long, long time before you were born'.

'I knew Granny Miller wasn't Dad's mother, but I don't seem to know anything about his real Mum. When did she die?'

My mother held up the dinner plate she was drying

and stared hard into its empty face.

'Oh it was years ago, our Dad was only a little boy. He never talks about it'.

'Gosh, I hadn't ever realised, in all these years'.

'Well you wouldn't. He never talks about it, your Dad'.

'So, what did she die of?' I asked and she stopped her slow circular drying.

She stiffened and stared down more intently. 'She done herself in. In the sea. Off the Nothe, I think'.

The Nothe! Where I had scrabbled as a child along the thin sunless strip of rock exposed at low tide, lifting dense, vile weeds in search of a mouthful of winkles to take home to boil for tea. The Nothe fort, a little beyond the tourist magnets of the beach and town, with ramparts and a sea wall, tunnels and heavy gates, there as a lumpen defence, we were instructed, against sea-borne invaders across the centuries.

My mother turned away from me towards the table, still holding the plate. Granny Miller had to somehow become a less established figure, as I tried to fit another woman, faceless and nondescript, into parts of her dominion. Somebody in a cart-wheeling trajectory against the sky, propelled from the top of the fortification onto the rocks.

'He's got a good brain on him, your Dad. He passed for the grammar when most of them, their parents had to pay. But then he had to leave after – when his mother - he had to go out to work to bring in some money'.

So much of it couldn't be right. I could not be learning about such happenings for the very first time at thirty six years of age. This violent, dramatic death was out of kilter with my whole sense of the past, with the pattern of people in a landscape, the threads and connections of family circumstance.

But there was no time for any further questions. My sons bundled into the room, still full of restless enthusiasm. 'Is it still switched on? Come on Grandma, we're all going to play'.

'Our Dad says I shouldn't have told you. I mustn't say anything else'.

She came straight out with it the following evening as soon as I dared raise the matter again. All day, at mealtimes, in the park, around the house as life adapted to the presence of new toys and their demands - furniture and schedules changed to accommodate the Spectrum - I had been struggling to hold the questions in, not to risk intense and furtive enquiries a few paces back behind the rest of the family.

'Dad says it was wrong to tell you. He won't talk about it'.

It didn't occur to me to wonder when this conversation between my parents had taken place. We had all been together in our holiday bustle almost all the time, with Dad and me sitting up late the previous evening drinking home-brewed beer, and Mum surely asleep by the time he and I made our whispering way upstairs. My mother and I could be interrupted again at any moment and a queasy awareness was growing that moments when family details could be exchanged had, in my life, been isolated between periods of silence somehow rigidly enforced over months and even years.

When the opportunity did arise to talk again, on that second evening clearing up after tea, I could think of no obvious or immediate questions. There was so much to re-configure, points of detail seemed potentially distracting and unhelpful. Instead I would have wished for the broad sweep of an account - pictures, words and colour - and, particularly, some explanation as to how I had never heard one hint or slip of the tongue, had never carried through my childhood even the faintest suspicion that, when the adults closed the doors, they communed together out of our earshot with secrets of such disruptive magnitude.

'Why did she do it? When was this, how old was Dad?'

'I don't know. All those children, I suppose. Four children and Grandad away at sea for most of the time. Dad was only a little nipper. He won't ever say anything about it'.

Four children and the back parlour, the room with the varnished panels, the stairs up into deep interiors that I had never seen and could not imagine, the outside toilet, the squashed-in back yard and the small strip of earth supporting Grandad's rows of vegetables. Granny Miller fitted there in Newbiggin Road with Grandad in a way that some new, indefinite presence would not. The lens could not focus and no defining outline would emerge from any amount of further facts and figures.

'What about your mother, then? I never knew her either, did I, but I do remember your Dad, Grandad Shergold?'

'Can you remember my father?'

Of course I remember him, I used to have my tea with him. But what about your mother? When did she die?'

'When you were little'.

'What of?'

The past I had never questioned or investigated, even in my fancies, was unrolling a sensational carpet right in front of me.

'She did it as well, didn't she? She did herself in!'

'She what? She did herself –'

'She did herself in. In the house where we lived, Purbeck Road. When you were a little nipper. They lived with us'.

'But how did she –'

'In the gas oven. Stuck her head in one morning. Before everyone was up. It was awful. I scrubbed and scrubbed but I could smell it for ages afterwards. It was in the walls. It was terrible, it made me feel sick. I don't like to think about it. Even now it makes me go all funny'.

How could any of this be true - one grandmother in the sea, another on the floor in the kitchen? All my mother's stories, all the family characters in a loosely-formed tableau, all my persistent questions as a child piecing together the links. We had been revisiting them for thirty-five years. How had we managed to weave around these two women, to sidestep them as we galloped or dawdled along? My mother would often lose herself in the stories, becoming gruesomely vivid and engrossing to me as a child. She re-lived the parts, sometimes became one character after the other, the events tumbling out beyond her control. Lost in another time and body, she would be pulled back into the present by my father. 'Steady on now, mother, come on'.

It seemed like a kindly, family joke. Well, almost. 'You were getting a bit carried away with yourself there'. My mother's animated account would die away and she would ease back into the room, returning to us far more subdued, offering perhaps a parting comment to her companions - 'a proper matelot he was' or 'poor old Granny'.

And then my sons came in one by one, drawn back to the Spectrum.

'Grandad says he wants a rest from Scrabble. '

'Are you ready for a go on the computer yet, Grandma? Grandad's going to read the paper for a while'

'Oh I don't think I can do that, my dears, I can't seem to get the hang of it'.

Why had it never occurred to me to wonder or to ask? If there were stepmothers, then there must have been mothers. It was obvious, but it was also an inaccessible thought. If this was true, then my father had lost his mother as a little boy, possibly with his own father on the other side of the world, far away at sea. There had never been one reference through all the years, no name, no slip of the tongue - no photograph. The things children shouldn't hear, I never heard. My curiosity had always pursued every corridor and room it encountered, there could be no locked door let alone a secret wing left unnoticed and unexplored.

Life could not possibly have been so ordinary. My parents could not have been the safe, predictable people they so clearly were, if any of this were true. I had been insulated from these deaths so completely by a protection almost chilling in its effectiveness. My mother offered nothing more, these huge family dramas from either side of the Second World War fading back into wherever it was that they were so securely accommodated. And yet that War itself had not been put to rest, it had been a daily talking point all through my growing up. I could feel no connection with the bereaved little boy in the panelled back room or the young woman in the tiny kitchen reeling from the sulphurous stench. This could not possibly be true. I could not have been so fundamentally wrong. I would have known. I would have had some inkling.

But there was no more time to question my mother, even if I could have found any focus and remained out of earshot of my sons. My father then walked into the kitchen carrying a small pile of empty plates that we had missed.

'This is what I like to see, people working. Don't stop on my account,' he said. 'Everybody alright out here then?'

'Oh yes, we're alright' my mother replied. 'We're just chatting'.

'Just putting the world to rights' I added, the words coming automatically.

'As long as everybody's alright, that's the main thing' he said, carefully inspecting the brown quart bottles with thickened glass necks and tightly secured stoppers that held in the final fermentation of my home brewed beer.

'I suppose it's a little too early for you, isn't it Andrew? What about you, Mam, not too early for you, is it?'

Neither Shape Nor Shadow

After my mother's revelations, my whole understanding of the rooms of our house in Weymouth had to stretch to accommodate another person, not some visitor at our door but an extra unsettled presence, my Mum's mother, already intimately within.

Neither shape nor shadow had remained. I had not retained the faintest remnant of a whisper, a cry or a sharp command. In our compact house, among the right angles, there were no corners or hideaways, no incubation spaces for disease, misery or secrets.

Somehow, if my mother's revelation was correct, a slumped human body had sprawled across our kitchen floor, an awful anonymity all around her despairing death, and then she was gone. No memory of brushing together in tight places, no waiting for an extra adult to take her turn, no prior claim on Grandad's attention and no disturbing of the peace. Somehow, the stories, the characters, the turnings of the year fitted perfectly together. There were no missing connections and no persisting hint of sulphur in my nostrils.

In 1987, after a professional conference in Bournemouth, I made a return visit to the Shorehaven estate. I parked in Cheviot Road around the corner from Purbeck Road and walked back and forth through the streets and lanes, weaving loops and patterns as I covered every familiar step, going nowhere in particular until I stood on the opposite side of the road looking at our old house. The privet hedge was gone, the garden paved over and open to the road to allow car parking.

All that work, our boundary with the outside world. Every leaf in the hedge had been kept in check, groomed as carefully as any stabled horse. The vegetables that fed us, the chrysanthemum petals in their thousands that my Dad seemed to inspect individually for signs of pests. Obliterated.

I wanted to march up and knock on the back door, to be shown around, to have my story acknowledged and to hear the history of the last twenty years. Instead I set off around the block, cutting in through The Rec, the huge municipal beasts having been replaced with smaller slides and swings, underlain with spongy safety materials. Around the block, down Pennine Road where I had walked to and from junior school twice a day, little seemed to have changed. Some gardens were scruffier. Nobody would have tolerated a waterlogged newspaper strewn across their front garden in my childhood years. But some also asserted self-improvement with small front porches and nameplates. The substance, however, was unchanged, the warm red bricks flaking only a little more, the tarmac road perhaps a little more substantial and less patched, the quiet pace of neighbourhood undisturbed.

I stood again opposite number 100, willing myself to knock the door. This was not a place I felt I could tarry. Strangers were still noticed. Everybody I had seen during my walking had been unfamiliar to me. I would feel foolish undertaking another lap. And then I was somehow knocking on the back door. How many times had I knocked on doors around here and then run away as a child? Please let there be nobody in. What was I doing? What would I say if somebody answered? I could still run away. And then I knocked again. No, no, no. Please let there be nobody at home.

I looked down at the backdoor step and the configurations flashed into place. The concrete oblong, the chipped corner, the slight scoop about the size of a penny, and another a bit smaller, the sheen of an embedded pebble and two other smaller ones beside it. Not a memory, not some impression distantly familiar. More a template, vital and right at the forefront of my mind but never fired or triggered through all the intervening years. The exact pattern – instantaneous recognition and delight rushing up through my body with an intensity that all the walking and other nostalgic musings of the day had come nowhere near to matching.

I had come right down to eye level with my soldiers on this step as a child. The saucer of milk had been placed at one end to tempt Timmy, the ginger tomcat from across the road. Prince, the mongrel from Mendip Road, had arrived here every morning one summer holiday, pawing the door to be let in before I was even out of bed. Arriving home from junior school in the winter, to tomato soup or occasionally a boiled egg from our neighbour's hens. Sitting out here in summer before Sunday lunch, the radio coming through the open kitchen door. Jean Metcalf in London and Bill Crozier in Cologne. 'From all of us over here to all of you over there'. BFBO. Brough and Archie Andrews. The Billy Cotton Band Show. My Dad, ready to carve the meat, appearing at the door to sharpen the knife. 'Come on now, let the dog see the rabbit' – my cue to move so that he could swish and scrape the blade back and forth, faster almost than the eye could see, scissoring the step.

'And if you can't find a partner, use a wooden chair, but let's Rock!'

I couldn't run and the door was opening. A man with a large belly, his vest swelling over the top of his partly unbuttoned trousers stood rubbing his eyes and trying to recognise me.

'I'm sorry. I was just passing and - um. I used to live

here'

'Used to live here? Come in. I'm sorry' he said scratching his dishevelled hair. 'I work Saturday mornings, I'm a plumber, and I have a drink lunchtimes. Come in. I was just sleeping. You must be – What's your name?'

I told him.

'That's right. There was that suicide. Your mother wasn't it?'

'My grandmother!' I forced out in alarm.

He knew. I was hardly back in the kitchen after twenty years and he had come straight out with it. I hadn't considered this aspect, somehow supposing that, when my mother had told me at Christmas a few years earlier, the catastrophe had been tidied away from everybody's memory in a day or two, that nobody else had paid it much attention if they had even noticed at all. But he'd blurted it out within seconds, whereas they had held it within themselves each and every day of the nineteen fifties and the nineteen sixties. Or, at least, in my presence they had.

Round the corner in Pennine Road, Aunt Hilda had known but I had never heard her speak. Across from her, Mrs Symons held sway, a woman not to get on the wrong side of, my father said. She sold toffee apples from her kitchen door around bonfire night, her Alsatian dog eyeing each of us customers as if making a mental record, and we knew not to complain that the sticks splintered in our mouths, or to try to see past her in case there were any bigger ones on the tray inside her kitchen. She had known. She had sons older than me, one of them, Shorty, not having been right in the head, my mother said, since he fell out of a tree collecting conkers on Southwell Avenue. He wouldn't have known, or at least he wouldn't have remembered after his accident, but his older brother might have. I admired Alan Symons, he was tall and confident and I used to watch him chasing girls with stinging nettles up at The Rec, threatening to brush their bare legs. He might just have been old enough to know.

Across the road from us, Mrs Devaney would have known. When I was in the sixth form I heard her expressing exaggerated surprise to my mother that I would be staying on at school for yet another year, her Robert being the same age and already half way through his apprenticeship. Next door to them, Mr and Mrs Shilitoe, marooned with their daughter Alice who had Down's Syndrome, kept their quiet counsel. And they had known. Boys sometimes congregated at their front gate and as Alice sat moon-faced at the window they shouted 'Monkey!' and put their hands to the sides of their temples, wriggling their fingers and making sounds of disgust. 'Poor Mrs Shilitoe, with that Alice. It's a shame,' my mother said, the source of the pity a daily presence.

Next door again, an old man we called Fogey Dyke, grumpy and red faced. One summer evening in my early teens, I led my brother across the road to his yellowing laurel hedge, armed with unwanted, over-ripe tomatoes. Once the first one had been thrown at his front door, we disgorged the rest with fire in our limbs, vulnerable now with our cache still in our hands, the soft thuds still falling, trails of juice and seeds sluicing down his door and walls. The neighbour who had observed us running back home and informed our father and old Fogey Dyke himself - they may both have known, they may have made allowances or taken quiet note of early slips into deviance.

Clive Varney's Dad, cycling past the house and whistling on his way to work, steering his bike with one hand. His loss, his other arm blown off in the War, was there for us all to see. Away from his cheerful progression along our road, in a garden shed or beside an allotment bonfire perhaps, he may have occasionally weighed his severed bone and flesh against a terrified exit from life by means of a gas oven.

Mary Brownlow, two houses down from Mrs Symons, gave me a lift on her Vespa scooter once or twice in my teens when we both worked on the bingo stall in the seafront amusement arcade. Like most of my neighbourhood contemporaries, swiftly through secondary modern school and out into work whilst I still walked to and from the grammar school through our estate in my blazer, cap and tie, her queries seemed to be without envy. 'Are you still squatting for exams?' she once yelled over her shoulder as we jumped a ragged gear change and wobbled with screaming revs into the attack on St Martin's Hill. Mary might not have known but, hemmed in behind a small front garden of wayward couch grass and wild barley - no hedge, just cast concrete posts and broken strands of rusty wire - her reclusive mother would have secreted this knowledge away somewhere in her gloomy living room.

But my brother and I heard no word, never a slip of the tongue nor a mysterious allusion. There was no malicious barb from the kids at The Rec, no overly condescending care or concern from the adults around us.

So, where and how had secrets been archived in these streets and houses? The immediate reference to the suicide showed that the trace was still charged and undimmed. The story was alive, the account still jumped the dislocations between person and time. The impact of the kitchen step, dull and ordinary but able to trigger an unstoppable carnival of colour and sound, screamed an unanswered challenge to the other doors that could be seen from our back step, as close and closed as they always had been.

The plumber opened the kitchen door wider.

'You'd better come in. I'm sorry, I'm still a bit asleep'

'No, I'm sorry. I really shouldn't have disturbed you. I was just walking by, visiting, and I thought – you know'.

'Do you want a cup of tea? How do you like it? It's a bit tricky tea isn't it, sometimes. I'll put the kettle on'.

There was no under stairs cupboard in the kitchen, no structure at all. Instead an alcove had been constructed and this now housed a small, bronze-topped telephone table and a stool. The walls were sculpted white in textured paint and the kitchen appeared at least twice its former size. I remembered that my mother had sometimes been sickened by the thought that a mouse was living in the boxes of junk at the very back of the cupboard and we had interacted only with items stored near the front.

'God. That used to be an under stairs cupboard, all that. My Grandad used to keep his...' and I was unable to speak, taken over by the life we had lived in that room.

'It's alright, son' he said, although he was little older than me. 'This tea'll be ready in minute. Got to let it boil though, haven't you? Do you want a look around?'

'Sharon!' he called and a young woman, blonde-haired and wearing jeans and a white T-shirt, appeared from the living room. 'This chap used to live here before us, before you were born. Show him around will you, while I sort this tea out'.

'Alright' she said 'but you haven't forgotten that I'm going out though, have you?'

I wanted to apologise again for intruding but I also wanted to be left alone to rummage, not to be escorted in what had been my own home, the place where all my childhood had been spent. Sharon too had lived almost all her life in 100 Purbeck Road shocking me from my assumption that, apart from my brother, I had to be the only person to have come from birth to adult independence here. She was casually territorial, while I stared into the bathroom, the toilet, and her bedroom, deeply severed from what had once been mine.

'It's just incredible that somebody else has... I mean, my whole childhood... I can't really...' I fumbled.

Sharon herself might well know. If so, had my grandmother's death become part of some spooky tale she relayed to her friends? Or did it elicit reserve and a quiet privacy?

'Dad!' she suddenly shouted, unsettling me as I must have unsettled her, ''I'm staying over at Kelly's tonight. You've remembered, right?' A blue holdall was lying open on her bed, curling tongs and a toilet bag showing through the half-zipped top. In my old bedroom, there was a dressing table and mirror, with lipstick, make-up, necklaces and earrings spilled across its surface.

My teachers! Had they all been aware of our circumstances? And doctors. Did they keep records of such things in their files back then?

'Tell that chap his tea's ready,' the man shouted and I welcomed the chance to join him back downstairs, away from rooms preserved for me in the mustiness of memory, the windows now flung wide and aired by youth and femininity. My brother and parents, my grandparents even more so, were no more than minor echoes in the last floorboard still to creak and in the stale atmospherics of awkward corners up near the ceiling. A new, careless modernity had usurped it all.

'I used to lie on that landing floor upstairs with our new transistor radio,' I told him 'Between the two main bedrooms. Trying to tune into Radio Luxembourg. My Dad said the reception was good because the electricity cables ran down inside those walls. It was the only chance to hear pop music most of the time.'

'You couldn't get the signal,' he said. 'Mind you, it's not much better now sometimes'.

Sometimes. Cliff Richard had sung '*Living Doll*' and the Beach Boys '*Barbara Ann*' with warm, rounded depths and razor-edged harmonies. But then the sound would fade becoming blunt and undernourished. Sometimes foreign languages, urgent and gabbling, would surge over the border, cutting across each other, growing louder and unchecked. At other times, I would attempt to tune the dial through an absolute minimum and be met by sounds from between the planets or the bleak anonymity of a Morse code signal, like some last message from a mass of black Atlantic rock, guano-caked and devoid of vegetation.

The tea was milky and very weak with a film on its surface.

'That alright for you?' he asked.

'Yes it's fine,' I replied. 'Thank you'.

Acknowledgements

The facilities and support provided by Nottingham Writers Studio have made the writing of this book a far more sociable enterprise than it would otherwise have been. In particular, I have enjoyed and benefited greatly from the critical insights of Paul Anderson, Gaynor Backhouse, Angela Barton, Megan Taylor and Frances Thimann. I am also extremely grateful to Alan Appleby, a school friend from sixty years ago (!), for permission to use his photographs for the cover.

HANGING IN THE BALANCE

Andy Christopher Miller

A collection of writing about survival in
relationships and climbing.

*'Who can say when or how hope springs? Today like a
ray of sunlight, a small book has landed on my desk ... It
may already be a collector's item ... For there is a breath
of humanity in this book ... Having this book in my
hands for half an hour was like sitting on the grass with
my back against a tree. It made me sway...'*

> Ed Drummond
> Poet, activist and leading
> British rock climber.
> In *Mountain*

*'This brave, fragile pamphlet of four essays and six
poems deftly tells the story of hanging in the balance as
climber, father, companion, husband, club-member and
divorcee. It begins with a crag rescue and ends with the
challenge of Christmas Day alone, 'without self-pity or
cynicism.' This is the best writing I've read for ages.
Better than whole books of empty narrative, this little
bit of autobiography climbs through the important
things in life. It will repay re-reading'.*

> Professor Terry Gifford
> Director of the International
> Festival of Mountaineering
> Literature
> In *High*

Amcott Press   Published 1988

WHILE GIANTS SLEEP

Andy Christopher Miller

Andy Miller's prose and poetry has won a range of awards and commendations. Daisy Goodwin, the judge for the 2011 international Yeovil Literary Prize, described him as having '. . . *a distinctive voice. . .*' and his prize-winning poem 'Attempting to Interfere' as being '. . . *mysterious but repaying a close reading*'. His long out-of-print booklet 'Hanging in the Balance' also attracted critical acclaim and is reprinted here in full. This new anthology displays a twin focus on mountaineering, rock climbing and outdoor adventure and on relationships across the adult life span.

'This collection pulses with life and energy ... Previously published and unpublished work spanning forty-two years is combined in this book, providing an intimate overview of a life lived on the edge in the most literal sense ... Miller's writing is sometimes humorous, deeply personal, and full of richly detailed observations, part of a continually developing tradition of walking and climbing literature'.

Aly Stoneman
Left Lion, Nottingham

Amcott Press   2nd Edition 2015

Printed in Great Britain
by Amazon.co.uk, Ltd.,
Marston Gate.